Still Running

By the same author

The Glasgow Gospel
A Scots Gospel
Auld Testament Tales
A Glasgow Bible
Will I Be Called an Author?
Proverbs in the Patter
A Counterblaste to Tobacco

STILL RUNNING

The Seven Lives of a
Glasgow Phenomenon

Jamie Stuart

SAINT ANDREW PRESS
Edinburgh

Published in 2014 by
SAINT ANDREW PRESS
121 George Street
Edinburgh EH2 4YN

Some of the content of this book has been published in *Will I Be Called an Author?*, ISBN 1-898169-17-9 (ISBN 978-1-898169-17-8)

Copyright © Jamie Stuart, 2014

ISBN 978-0-86153-858-4

British Library Cataloguing in Publication Data
A catalogue record for this book is available from the British Library.

It is the publisher's policy to only use papers that are natural and recyclable and that have been manufactured from timber grown in renewable, properly managed forests. All of the manufacturing processes of the papers are expected to conform to the environmental regulations of the country of origin.

Typeset by Regent Typesetting

Printed and bound in the United Kingdom

Contents

Acknowledgements

I am deeply grateful to my family and friends who supported me in the planning of this book. In particular, I want to thank my daughter Fiona and my granddaughter Gillian for spending so many hours typing, e-mailing, and checking my spelling. God has blessed me with many friends who encouraged me. They include: Douglas Elliott, May Fawns, Robert Fernie, Telford George, Agnes Logan, Mary McLeod, Catherine Smillie and Margaret Wallace. My head of publishing at Saint Andrew Press, Ann Crawford, and my editor, Ivor Normand, have been very patient with me. The idea for the book came from my mentor, Donald Smith. I hope he approves.

Foreword

This is a story of Glasgow over nearly 100 years. It bears witness to the city's people and to the ever-changing backdrop of history.

But rising above the history is the spirit of Glasgow, and in particular of a talented lad, Jimmy Stuart – wee Ginger, or now Jamie. He has talent and a bit of get-up-and-go. He has no special privileges; he has to take his knocks with the rest, and some of them are 'sair dunts'. Yet, every time, he picks himself up and has another go. Is this not the story of Glasgow?

There is a restlessness here as well. Jamie Stuart could claim to have had seven lives. He has been an athlete, actor, airman, salesman, social worker, author and evangelist. For Jamie, there is always a new challenge, another hill to climb, even if nowadays it is with the help of two skilfully replaced knees!

It could have been a disaster – at several points, it almost was – but two things have given Jamie Stuart the will to keep going. One is his sense of humour, evident throughout these pages. In Jamie's hands, even the Bible can be a source of fun and laughter – as his best-selling *The Glasgow Gospel* shows.

The other thing, underpinning all, is his Christian faith and commitment. At key moments in this story, you find Jamie Stuart turning to God, not as a distant idea but as a present help and support. Thousands of ordinary Glaswegians will testify to that.

I appear late in his story because the enthusiasms of a young theatre director and an aspirant author sparked off each other, to put Jamie's *A Scots Gospel* on stage, on tour and in print. It has been a privilege and an inspiration to work with this wee man – but don't let on I told you. Glasgow Jamie is truly a Glasgow witness, and in later years he has become an ambassador not just for his native city but also for Scotland.

PROFESSOR DONALD SMITH
Director, The Scottish Storytelling Centre

Psalm 1

Blythe is the bodie who shuns the guidin o the ungodly,
An who doesnae hing oot wi sinners.
His hert's joy lies wi God's biddin,
An he ponders it baith day an nicht.

He'll be like a tree staunin firm by the watter,
Producin guid fruit in season
Wi nae deid leaves tae be seen.
But the sinners are like chaff blawin aboot in the wind.

They'll have nae chance on the Day o Judgement,
Banished frae the guid folk.
For God kens weel the gate o the Righteous;
The gate o the wicked will fade awa.

1

Early Days

The midwife smiled. My wee naked body was safely delivered into her eager hands. There had been no stress – but yes, some blood, sweat and tears. Let me tell you about the tears.

The date was 10 September 1920. I had two brothers – John and Peter – six years and three years old respectively. My mother had always been desperate for a girl, and hoped fervently that the good Lord would answer her prayer. Surely number three would meet her heart's desire?

'Well now, Mrs Stuart,' said the midwife, 'you can have a shot now, there you are, lassie – a lovely big boy!' Hear this! My mother burst into tears and wept uncontrollably for several minutes.

Dr McNab came forward. 'Dear me! Dear me! What's all this carry-on about, Mrs Stuart? What's vexing you?'

'I'm fine, Doctor,' my mother replied, blowing her nose furiously, 'but you see, I wanted a wee girl this time.' And the wailing increased in volume.

'Mrs Stuart,' said the Doc, 'you should be ashamed of yourself. We've had no trouble at all; you have at your bosom a lovely healthy boy. He looks great. I'll tell you this – you are the mother of a prize baby!'

In later years, my mother, bless her heart, regretted telling me the story of my entry into the world. Whenever she had cause to reprimand me for any reason, I would remind her that I was her Prize Baby! This usually prompted a smart scud in the behouchie, and I would get the message! (By the way, the final addition to the family was also a boy!)

Fortunately for me, the message I received in childhood was one of love and devotion from committed Christian parents. My father was born in Tobermory on the Isle of Mull and arrived in Glasgow as a 14-year-old with his widowed mother. My mother was born in Glasgow's Gorbals and married my father in 1913. Born in 1920, I completed the 'Trio of Apostles', Peter, James and John. Three years later, Ronald was born; I can't remember why he wasn't christened Andrew. My birthplace was 48 Kingarth Street in the Crosshill district of Glasgow, very near the centre of the city, but I have virtually no memory of my first five years living there.

In 1925, things were looking up for my dad. He was in full charge of the warehouse of Thomson and Mathieson Ltd, fruit brokers, merchants and importers at 40 Ingram Street, Glasgow, and had been employed with the firm for twelve years. He reckoned that his job was secure, and he had managed to save a bit of money. Leaving the city, he took his wife and four boys into the country – into a pleasant village called Stepps, just ten miles away. The address was MarieVille, Alexandra Avenue; our bungalow was at the foot of the avenue. We had a huge garden and an unrestricted view of the countryside. Life was good. John Stuart from Tobermory had made it! He created a lovely garden filled with an array of trees, shrubs and heathers. At the back, we had all kinds of vegetables, plus two white rabbits and a dozen hens, so there was no shortage of freshly laid eggs. Along with my brothers, Jack and Peter, I attended the local primary school just ten minutes away via the shortcut past the tennis courts. On Sundays, Mum and Dad marched proudly to the Church of Scotland in Blenheim Avenue with their four sons.

At the bottom of our avenue, the Girl Guides had a small wooden hut. It was situated in a field directly across from our house, and I can well remember being spellbound when seeing my first-ever concert in that place. To a seven-year-old, it was magic indeed – accordions, fiddles, dancing, singing and recitations. The atmosphere must have had an effect on

2

me; in due course, I spent some years as a thespian 'treading the boards'. Interestingly enough, about 150 yards from the Guides' Hut (it's still there) is the Parish Church of Stepps. In January 1999, I was invited to their annual Burns Supper to recite 'Holy Willie's Prayer' and *Tam o' Shanter*. Memories of the Guides' concert seventy years earlier kept drifting back.

In the summer, we explored 'the Wee Wood' and the North Woods. The local farmer allowed us to ride on the hay-carts at harvest time. My brothers and I enjoyed good health, and I think we were reasonably well behaved, although I do recall a time when we raised the ire of my dad. The four of us shared a room – and one night (about midnight) we engaged in a very competitive pillow fight. It would appear that it got out of control, because I remember my dad turfing the four of us out of the house in our pyjamas onto the cold, wet grass until we cooled down.

For holidays, Dad bought a big tent, and we went camping at Balmaha on the banks of Loch Lomond. We scaled Ben Lomond, stayed to see the sunrise and felt on top of the world.

My mother was a small lady, five feet and one inch tall. We all loved her dearly – and why not? She was the most gentle and caring of people, and I honestly cannot remember her losing her temper, although with four energetic sons I'm sure she must have had cause. Anyway, I remember her as a kindly mother and an able parent. She played the piano and sang sweetly, was a super cook and a good baker. Her smile was pure gold; she laughed a lot and enjoyed reading Annie S. Swan in *The People's Friend*. Our family was blessed with two caring and disciplined parents who led by example. Dad earned £5 per week in 1926, which I guess would have been an above-average wage. He was a gifted handyman, and personally made the beds we slept in. He also equipped himself with shoemaker's tools and repaired the footwear for all six of the family. We didn't go into Glasgow city centre very much as a family, but I have a memory of visiting a pantomime at the Princess' Theatre in the Gorbals (now the Citizens' Theatre) and seeing the popular comedian George West in a show. It was great value in those days: the pantomimes lasted for four hours! I remember my parents taking us to Green's Cinema in Renfield Street (at that time the biggest cinema in Europe) and seeing Charles Laughton and Norma Shearer in *The Barretts of Wimpole Street*. I also have a glimmer of a memory of being taken to Hengler's Circus in Sauchiehall Street. The great comedy attraction was Doodles the Clown, who always seemed to get wrapped up in the carpet. Also, there was a most spectacular water scene, which of course flabbergasted the children present.

On 26 October 1926, my father suffered a cruel blow, one from which he never fully recovered. On that day, as he left work, he was given a letter:

Dear John,

I regret that we are unable to keep you on in our employment at the wage you are receiving, and we would prefer if you would look out for another situation commencing Monday 8 November.

If you would rather stay on here, it could only be at a weekly wage of £2 10s.

Yours faithfully
J. H. THOMSON

Dad was obliged to seek another job. On 12 November, he received a reference from Thomson and Mathieson Ltd:

To WHOM IT MAY CONCERN

The bearer, Mr John Stuart, was in our employment for a period of about twelve years. He acted at first as a Dispatch Clerk to our Travellers' Department, and latterly he was in full charge of our Warehouse. In both these positions we found him to be thoroughly reliable and trustworthy, and we have pleasure in recommending him to anyone who requires an efficient and competent warehouseman.

Yours truly,
Robt. R. Allan
Managing Director

The story goes that Dad's employer wanted to place a family member in Dad's position – and so my honest, hard-working father was sacrificed. In later years, he confided in me: 'James, I sat with my head in my hands in George Square and wondered what on earth I was going to do!'

It must be realised that, in 1926, the economy was not buoyant and a depression was imminent. In May of that year, the trade unions empowered the General Council of the TUC to call a National Strike to support the miners. They had been locked out by the mine-owners after refusing to accept wage cuts and changed conditions. A mile from our house, across the fields, soldiers with fixed bayonets stood guard at the pit-head of Cardowan Colliery. Transport workers, railwaymen, dockers, printers and industrial workers throughout the country stopped work. There were no newspapers. Industry was paralysed, and the government refused to move. The strike lasted for nine days. The Wall Street Stock Exchange crash of 1929 produced world-wide misery and triggered what was called the Great Depression, which lasted until the mid-1930s. This was a period of low output and investment, with high unemployment. Times were bad in the UK; in the USA, they were a disaster!

During 1932, the worst year of the Depression, 34,000,000 Americans were without any income. Thousands of people, unable to find even a soup kitchen, rummaged for food among the garbage. In country districts, they ate weeds. A popular song of that time was 'Buddy, can you spare a dime?' about a man who had helped to build the American dream and now found himself begging in the street. My dad hired a horse and cart, bought fruit and vegetables from the market, and for the next five months tried to make a living selling his produce round the streets of Stepps. Unfortunately, he wasn't cut out to be an outside trader, and he often ended up giving his stock away for nothing rather than dumping it. On 13 April 1927, he became employed as an agent with the Scottish Legal Life Assurance Society, and he remained with that Society until his retirement in 1949, aged 65.

In 1929, we couldn't afford to remain in Stepps and were obliged to move. It must have been a traumatic time for my folks, but at nine years of age the reality of the situation did not affect me. I trusted my parents implicitly and felt that all would turn out well. We packed up our goods and chattels and settled in Carntyne in the East End of Glasgow, in a four-in-a-block council house in Carntyne Road. A few years later, we moved to a semi-detached house in Edinburgh Road, Carntyne, once more with our own gate and large garden.

2

Bible Exam

I am still living in this house and attend High Carntyne Parish Church, just around the corner. I'm an elder in the kirk, and also the Prayer Secretary. The Church came into being in 1930, in a large wooden hut that was the property of the 162nd Boys' Brigade Company. The Reverend Robert Kirkland conducted the first service of worship on Sunday 30 March 1930. More than twenty people attended, and we have a record of the offering at that historic service: £1 13s 9d (£1.68). On hearing about a Sunday School for young folk attached to High Carntyne Church, I enrolled immediately, as I didn't want to repeat the embarrassment I had suffered one year earlier in Stepps Village Church. Here's the story of that episode in my young life.

I expect that most of us want to be good at something – to be an achiever. Success in one's life and in general relationships is surely a common goal. My earliest recollection of trying to succeed (and to win a prize!) in an exam was a disaster. Each Sunday that God sent, I had to satisfy my mum and dad that the back of my neck and ears were scrubbed, my ginger hair was slicked down and my boots were well polished. The bells were ringing; Mr and Mrs Stuart and family made their way to the kirk.

For some reason or other, I was not a member of the Sunday School. I've no doubt my parents were busy enough coping with life in those hard times. Our only connection with the Church was the Sunday morning service, and I didn't think to question my parents about Sunday School. Church attendance was a great joy for me. I loved the atmosphere and the dignity of all concerned. The sermons were long, and I certainly didn't understand them, but my attention was alerted one year when the Sunday School Bible Exam prizes were presented. I decided that I too would be fair proud to step up to the front of the kirk and receive a prize. The following spring, a pulpit intimation was read out stating that the Bible exams would be held in the church hall on the first Saturday of the next month at 3pm. I was eight years old. I desperately wanted to win a prize and to shake hands with the minister's wife.

The important day arrived, and I reported at the church hall. The teachers seemed surprised to see me. Who could blame them? I wasn't a member of the Sunday School and had not received even a vestige of instruction or preparation to equip me for the test. Even so, I was directed to a desk, upon which lay several sheets of white paper, a pen and a pot of ink. At one minute to three, the question paper was handed out, and at three o'clock sharp the bell was rung. My first action was dead easy. I wrote my name and age at the top of the first sheet. I read the first question and realised I couldn't answer it; likewise the second question, and the third, and so on to the end of the paper. I was totally out of my depth. I knew nothing. The other boys and girls were writing away furiously. I blew my nose for something to do. My face was hot. I could feel it burning. My head was bursting. I was in agony. The tears splashed onto the virgin paper – well, not quite; it had my name and age on it.

A teacher noticed my torment and quietly asked if I was not well. I mimed to her that I had a headache – and, without making eye contact with anyone, I tip-toed to the door. Outside, I breathed the fresh air of an escaped prisoner. My mum and dad knew nothing of my doings, and I never informed a living soul about that sorry day.

3

Carntyne

Arriving in Carntyne in 1929, I seemed to make the transition from the rural atmosphere of Stepps to the outskirts of the big city of Glasgow with the greatest of ease. Along with my pals, I went on the rowing boats at Hogganfield Loch and played pitch-and-putt and golf at Lethamhill golf course. I joined everything – the swimming baths, the library, the dramatic societies and the junior choir. I wasn't particularly interested in girls, but I do remember noting that there was a certain choir member called May Kelt who was most attractive.

We climbed trees and played cricket. There weren't many cars or buses around at that time, and I recall that we played football in the middle of Carntyne Road – on home-made stilts! I went through the various departments of our church Sunday School – primary, junior, intermediate and senior, plus the junior and senior Bible classes. In the early 1930s, Carntyne was a burgeoning housing scheme containing many families. High Carntyne Church boasted the largest Sunday School in Scotland – 1,000 pupils and 100 teachers.

The church was the hub of the community, and its minister the Reverend Tom Crichton was the life and soul of the church. His ministry began in 1930 and lasted until 1948. He was a First World War veteran, having lost a leg in the conflict. However, his disability did not affect his ministry, and he made good use of his Baby Austin car to get around the parish.

The annual Sunday School summer trip was a big occasion in the lives of the young folk. In the early 1930s, we did not travel to the location by bus or train, probably because of the cost involved. Lorries were borrowed from the local farmer or coal-man. Clydesdale horse-power was used, and the animals were dressed up to the nines – gleaming brass ornaments on their harnesses and the most colourful and elaborate decorations on their tails. They were equine wonders to behold. Banners, flags, balloons and streamers disguised the lorries. The girls wore pretty dresses and ribbons in their hair. The boys wore white shirts and white sannies (plimsolls). In those days, we didn't travel very far; usually to a large field a few miles away from the church, with enough space to run the races and play five-a-side football. Margaret Smith, former Session Clerk of the Kirk, has a vivid memory of one of the early summer trips. Arriving at the chosen field, our eager Margaret started to run – and slipped, in her white dress, full length, onto a large cow-pat. Ever ready to accept the challenge, Mr Crichton helped Margaret into his car and drove the few miles back to Carn-tyne. Mrs Smith got the lass into a bath and into another dress, and they drove back to the fun and games.

Sunday School parties at Christmas were always happy occa-sions, although one of the Junior Department's regular games was of doubtful popularity. Many of the boys hid in the toilets when Bee Baw Babbity was announced. Silly boys! I was all for it – a kissing game. The teachers would round up as many lads and lassies as were willing, and circles were formed with everyone holding hands. A boy would be placed in the centre of the circle. The pianist then struck up the tune, and we moved clockwise singing 'Bee Baw Babbity, Babbity, Babbity, Bee Baw Babbity, kiss a bonny wee lassie'. At this point, the boy would select a girl, give her a peck and the girl would then go into the centre – and so on. It was very daring, and is my first memory of a collision with a girl's lips. Rena Morgan was in the centre of the ring and, on cue, chose me for a cheeper. She was a pretty girl. Eighty-four years on, we keep in touch and she's still a cracker.

I worked hard at my preparation for Bible exams and began a hobby of aiming for prizes. I joined the Life Boys and in due course was promoted to the Boys' Brigade. My memories of service with the 162nd Company of the Boys' Brigade are bittersweet. Certainly – in the main – I give thanks for the Christian fellowship I enjoyed, for learning the importance of discipline, for the athletic training and for all the fun and games. I earned the major award of the Boys' Brigade – the King's Badge – and was fair proud to wear it on my arm. As a 14-year-old, I won the Glasgow Battalion Mile Championship, and was looking forward to defending my title when an upset happened in my BB career. Looking back on the incident, I can smile, but I must have been a sorry lad at the time. Ye see, I told a wee lie! Well, that's not quite accurate. It wisnae a wee lie. It was a gey big lie!

One Friday evening, I requested to be excused from drill squad, complaining of a sprained ankle. I was really all right, and the following day I won a three-mile cross-country race. Next Friday, however, a shock awaited me. Over 100 boys were standing in the ranks. *Without any previous warning to me, without any meeting, or hint of any kind*, the captain of the Company made the following announcement: 'Now boys, I have something serious to say. Last week, one of our boys told a lie, and I'm sorry to say that the person involved is one of our best lads.' I was a corporal at the time and was staggered by what followed.

'The boy I refer to is Corporal James Stuart. As punishment, he will lose his stripes and return to the ranks.'

Certainly I deserved to be reprimanded – but to be reduced to the ranks? I felt cheated, and I've no regrets about my response. Without any hesitation, I marched smartly down the hall and up onto the platform, removed my belt and my lanyard and deposited them on the captain's table. 'Sir, I resign from the Company,' I said, and walked off home. I was not contacted, and of course lost my mile title since I could not defend it.

It's a funny old world, isn't it? And it's ironic that I'm now invited to be guest of honour at Boys' Brigade inspections and to adjudicate their Bible exams.

I completed my primary-school education at Riddrie School, passed my qualifying exam and went to Whitehill Secondary School. Alas, my secondary-school education did not win me any prizes. I could make my excuses: each morning I was up at 6am doing a paper round, and in the evenings I neglected my homework for training with Carntyne Amateur Athletics Club. As a result of these activities, I often fell asleep in class. As a member of the school drama club, I remember performing in the City Hall, and I also ran well in the annual sports meetings, but as a student I was not a success. In fact, I was obliged to repeat my second year of studies, and left school at 15. My father thought it was a good idea, and I didn't argue with him.

4

Going to the Dogs

My first job was as an office boy at a flour and grain merchant's office – John Richmond Ltd in McAlpine Street near Anderston Cross. I hated it. The chief clerk bullied me, and I determined on the first day that I would give it a trial but vowed there and then that I would not remain for more than one year.

As the deadline date drew near, I applied for a position as a salesman in Charles Rattray & Co., the well-known whole-sale warehouse in Candleriggs. My interview was successful, and I was assigned to the blanket department – at a pay of 30 shillings (£1.50) per week. In John Richmond's, I had been earning 10 shillings (50p) per week. I felt like a millionaire! I was fair pleased to give in my notice at John Richmond Ltd. The boss informed me that he had actually been considering giving me a pay rise and that he was sorry to lose me. His name was Mr Gibson. The clerk and I nicknamed him Hoot Gibson after the popular cowboy actor in the Hollywood films of that time. Come to think of it – Mr Gibson was a cowboy right enough!

My mum was delighted for me. She would take the pound note, and I would keep the 10 shillings for pocket money. Life was good. In fact, so good that one night I nearly 'went to the dogs' both literally and metaphorically. Let me explain. Some of my pals were keen to sample the thrills of gambling at Carntyne Greyhound Stadium, one mile from where I lived, and I went along with them. The stadium had recently opened and was one of the first to be built in the city. It was a novelty for the Glasgow gamblers, and they flocked to it like bees to a honeypot. In fact, the stadium owners were so keen to keep the customers dry on wet days that they erected a covered walkway about half a mile long which stretched from the tramcar stop in Duke Street and led right up to the turnstile entrance. There were programme-sellers, bookies, tipsters, tick-tack men and hot pie stalls. The meeting started at 6pm on a Friday – pay day. In possession of my envelope containing my precious 30 shillings, and straight from work, I joined my friends, knowing that I had 10 shillings to stake. After six races, I had lost the lot. I was not a happy wee boy. I thought of George Raft, the Hollywood film star who always seemed to be losing thousands of dollars in the gambling casinos. A gambler always wants to recoup his losses. I took a mad risk. I staked 10 shillings of my mum's pay in race seven. No luck! I could almost feel my father's heavy hand on the back of my head and on my backside.

There was one race left. Six dogs were on view. The race favourite was the Scottish greyhound champion, by the name of Ballycurreen Soldier. In my opinion, this dog could not lose. He was a lovely animal and very popular. The odds were 2 to 1. Nervously I went to the betting window. I surrendered the rest of my mother's cash on the counter. 'Ten shillings on Ballycurreen Soldier to win,' I whispered. There was a lot of running and shouting as last bets were placed. The tote windows were slammed shut as the six healthy, eager greyhounds were led into the traps. The punters crossed their fingers as the stadium lights were switched off and searchlights lit up the track. The bell rang and the backers bellowed. The electric hare wheeched off – and, by jings, Ballycurreen Soldier wheeched off in hot pursuit. He romped home the winner by five lengths. Wee Jimmy went home with his 30 bob back in his pocket. It was a salutary lesson nearly 'going to the dogs'.

I worked for two years with Rattray's and then moved into gents' outfitting. The shop at the corner of Buchanan Street and St Vincent Street was a gents' store for many years. In 1939 it was Watson's Ltd, and my boss was Mr Sam Vickery. He was a tall, strapping, smart gentleman in a check suit, bright waistcoat and bow tie, and with a curly moustache. He dined at Danny Brown's just round the corner in St Vincent Street.

Danny Brown's Restaurant is no more, but in 1940 it was one of the most prestigious eateries in the city, frequented by prosperous business people. Sam Vickery rubbed shoulders with bankers, lawyers and entrepreneurs. It was a 'place to be seen', and Mr V seemed expert in being chummy and passing round cigars. Needless to say, patrons of Danny Brown's often called at Watson's Ltd to purchase top-of-the-range shirts and suits at the top market prices.

In the early part of 1940, a dozen Polish seamen rolled into the shop. Their ship had been sunk, and a British vessel had rescued them. After having disembarked at Greenock, they made their way to what was probably an office of the exiled Polish government in Glasgow – and, armed with a wad of notes, they arrived in Buchanan Street on a freezing cold day.

They wore makeshift attire and were in need of warm overcoats. Only one of them spoke a little English. They were extremely subdued, friendly and very courteous. The spokesman proudly introduced himself to me with a name something like Vladek Bienkovsky. I think he was the captain. 'We want to buy big coats,' he smiled. 'Today in Glasgow it is – how you say? Bloody cold!' I agreed with him about the weather and took the crew below decks, leaving the junior assistant to man the reception area. The boss had just left for Danny Brown's.

We had a large stock of winter overcoats, so it was easy for me to fit out all the sailors. However, there was great merriment as I struggled to find one for a large sailor (probably the ship's cook) who must have weighed about 17 stone. An outsize Crombie coat soon covered his massive frame, and he strutted about like a model to great applause from his mates. I noted all the prices on one receipt, and Mr Vladek paid the bill. Upstairs, each man ceremoniously shook my hand as he left the shop. I had secured my biggest sale ever, and I wished them plain sailing.

Stuffing the crisp new notes into the till, I eagerly awaited the return of my employer. Having had his roast beef and a glass or two of wine, Mr V breezed in. He always made straight for the till to check the sales. His eyes popped. I got a bonus and the rest of the afternoon off.

5

Molly Urquhart

I think, really, that the acting bug first bit me when, as a nine-year-old, I was cast in a short play produced by the Life Boys (the junior section of the Boys' Brigade). I only had half a dozen lines to spout, but I remember making the most of them. I still have the script. From then on, I joined every amateur dramatic club that I could find: my own church club, various other church drama clubs, the Boys' Brigade concert party, the Whitehill School Society and the Lyric Players based in the YMCA in Sauchiehall Street.

Then it happened. I met Molly Urquhart! For an ambitious young would-be actor, it was a golden opportunity. Born and brought up in Glasgow, Molly decided not only to be an actress but also to establish her own theatre. She accomplished both of these aims triumphantly. As an actress, she was one of the stalwarts of the Glasgow Citizens' Theatre, made television appearances in *Dr Finlay's Casebook*, and went on to become internationally successful as a film actress.

In 1939, aged 33, Molly founded her own theatre in an old church hall in Rutherglen, and christened it the MSU Theatre, after her own initials. It was later to become the Rutherglen Repertory Theatre.

So it was that in August 1940, at age 19, I got the chance I had been waiting for. Coming home from work on the bus one night, I read about the MSU in Mamie Crichton's theatre column in the *Glasgow Evening News*. Hotfooting it the same night to Main Street, Rutherglen, I bowled into the theatre.

Rehearsal was in progress – and, at the first break, Molly herself came down to speak to me.

'Good evening,' I smiled hopefully. 'My name's James Stuart. I'm from Carntyne. I've just been reading in tonight's *Evening News* about your company, and I wonder if I could have an audition?'

'Well, you've got a famous name, young man. The big chap in Hollywood's done well for himself.' She put her arm round my shoulder and walked me down to the stage. 'Now, James Stuart, it just happens that I need one more actor to complete my cast for the particular play that we've started rehearsing. This is James Stuart, folks,' she announced to the players on the stage. 'Right, James.' Molly handed me a script. 'Your character is Mr Blow. You appear on page three. You're a loud-mouthed reporter, so belt it out, son.' It was a great wee part. I belted it out – and that was my baptism into the MSU.

My time with Molly's 'Good Companions' lasted for one whole season, and I appeared in every production. On reflection, I realise that I was involved in what was probably the most unusual theatrical venture ever undertaken in the UK.

The MSU existed for four years – the worst years of the Second World War – under the leadership of Molly Urquhart. The company consisted of twelve regular members. Nearly all of them held down jobs during the day. They were teachers, office workers, sales people, printers, bankers and the like. It was classed as a semi-professional theatre company. By that, I mean that we received our bus fares to get to the theatre – and not much more. We joined to learn stagecraft, for the joy of acting and for the experience of being part of an exciting adventure. Members were recruited from the ranks of various amateur clubs in and around Glasgow – but, on joining the MSU, one became a professional in every possible way.

In the four years of its existence, no fewer than ninety-seven three-act plays were produced, fifteen of them world premieres! How was it done? In the first week of the month, we would rehearse a production. In the second week, we would present the play, Monday to Saturday. In the third week, another play would be rehearsed and presented the following week, and so on. How was all this achieved? The cast met at the theatre on a Sunday afternoon. The play would be cast, and a full reading would take place; the first act would be moved in a rough fashion, and we would go home to mug up our lines for Act I. Full rehearsal of Act I would take place on Monday night. On the Tuesday, Act II would be moved and we would go home to learn our lines, to return on Wednesday for a full rehearsal of Act II. On Thursday, Act III would be set and memorised for rehearsal on Friday night. Sometimes we had a Saturday as a free day. During the Sunday, from 10am, very often until midnight, we would rehearse, rehearse, rehearse and have costume fittings and, at around 7pm, the final dress rehearsal.

The theatre only held 250 people, but on several occasions the House Full signs were on display. Many of the plays received glowing reviews from the press; and the critics made their way from London for important productions. Nevertheless, because it was a completely independent enterprise, Molly had to consider her budget very carefully. She worked – as did her team – on all aspects of the running of the theatre. We knocked on doors all over Rutherglen selling tickets for the events. We took turns in the box office. We scrubbed floors, painted scenery and created costumes. Versatility was the watchword.

On the late afternoon of a certain opening night, Molly was by herself scrubbing out the foyer when a group of reporters arrived and enquired of the charlady the whereabouts of Miss Urquhart.

'Haud oan therr a minute, son, an ah'll see if she's in,' said Molly – and she went off to the dressing room, changed her clothes and her accent and gave them their interview.

In view of all the demands placed upon the cast, and especially on Molly herself, there were times when it was impossible to be word-perfect. One Friday evening, Molly was on stage with Andrew Crawford. It was freezing weather, and the heating had broken down. This affected Molly, and she was having difficulty remembering her lines for one particularly long speech. However, she had secreted the prompter in the fireplace. Gliding upstairs in a dramatic movement, she had a prolonged discussion with the prompter to get her lines right again.

One reviewer commented on a heavy drama: 'I thought ... that the invalid's bed in the final act was badly placed'. The placing of the bed had been dictated by the fact that the director/manager/charlady/actress had been too hard pressed to memorise all the lines of the last act, and Margaret Smith the prompter was tucked under the bed!

Molly directed every production and frequently took one of the leading roles. She was a terrific driving force and was instrumental in launching young actors into professional careers. Molly inspired many Scottish actors, including Gordon Jackson, Stanley Baxter, Duncan Macrae, Rona Anderson, Eileen Herlie and Nicholas Parsons.

6

Airman

In the summer of 1940 as a 19-year-old, I knew that it would not be long until I was called up to the Forces. So, at the beginning of June, I volunteered to join the RAF. The recruiting officer's question caught me off guard. 'Would you like to train for ground-crew duties or for air crew?' As I hesitated, he mentioned that there was more money as an air-crew trainee. It was suggested that I would be a suitable candidate for wireless operator/air-gunner training. I took the bait, as I expected that the war would be over before the end of my training. What a hope!

By 1941, RAF training camps had sprung up all over Scotland and England. Most of those camps were situated well away from civilisation, from shops, theatres, cinemas, dance halls – and girls. The initial months of service were marked by hours of square-bashing, rifle-drill and physical exercises in order to get the rookies into shape to face up to the Nazi menace.

On call-up, where was I posted to in sunny June '41? To Blackpool! To civilian digs. I had 'won a watch' indeed. Kathleen from Halifax arrived on holiday and stayed in the top floor of our billet. All residents shared the dining room, and a harmonious time was had by all. Sure, we had all the tedium of countless hours of drill, but on most evenings we were free to dance at the Tower Ballroom and the Winter Gardens – all for sixpence (2½p)!

During the day, along with hundreds of other prospective wireless operators/air gunners, I was taught the intricacies of Morse code. Burton's spacious clothing shops and warehouses were taken over as classrooms, and many trainees failed as the speed progressed from five words a minute up to thirty words a minute.

Chambers' dictionary gives the definition of 'gone for a Burton' as airmen's slang meaning drowned, dead, absent or missing. It has been suggested that the phrase was originally coined after an airman failed the Morse code tests at Burton's.

In the daytime, I tapped away with my Morse code buzzer, and in the evenings I waltzed the night away on the dance floor with Kathleen. Did I fall in love with this winsome Yorkshire lass? Of course I did. Walking home one moonlit night, we sang the popular song of the time, *Amapola*, and vowed that, at any time in the future when we heard *Amapola* played, we would think of each other. We kept in touch for a while; then she married a soldier, and we wished each other well.

On completion of my wireless-operator training at Blackpool, I was posted to a small transmitting station near Invergordon in northern Scotland to await my gunnery course. During this time, I served as a crew member on Sunderland flying boats. The Sunderland was developed from the Short C-class flying boat that had been built in 1936 for Imperial Airways. Before the war, it was used for carrying passengers and mail across the Atlantic and to the Commonwealth countries. Equipped with front and rear gun turrets, as well as port and starboard gun positions, it could carry bombs and depth charges. It was a most useful aircraft for offensive and reconnaissance missions. Twelve-hour sorties and a crew of twelve made the galley retained from the civil aircraft a most welcome addition. Sunderland crews were always well fed. The Germans called the Sunderlands the 'Porcupines' because of their all-round firepower, and had a great respect for them.

After Invergordon, there was a posting to Yatesbury in Wiltshire for more wireless training. Then on to Pembrey in Wales for air-gunner training; and in due course I arrived in Ashbourne, Derbyshire as a fully qualified wireless operator/ air gunner. At Ashbourne OTU (Operational Training Unit), I joined an air crew and trained for several months prior to being posted to Thruxton, an operational squadron in Hampshire in the south of England. So, there I was – ready, willing and waiting to face the enemy.

Then something unusual happened which very probably saved my life. After only one week at the 'ops' squadron, and without being used on any missions, our entire air crew was returned to Ashbourne OTU. We were informed that, until further notice, we would be required as instructors, as there was a desperate shortage of 'screens'. The posting back to Ashbourne was a mixed blessing. Most of the instructors at the unit were 'operation-hardened' and experienced fliers, having done one or more tours of operation, and as a reward they were 'screened' from further operations for a period of time and were posted to the training units to instruct the rookies.

So, here I was, a 'screen' – far away from the enemy, instructing the new recruits – without ever having seen action myself. Nevertheless, I was also obliged during that time to join a crew as a wireless operator with pilots flying solo for the first time. This was hazardous in the extreme and with no chance of a medal for bravery. I flew with at least three sorry young pilots who crash-landed their aircraft and failed the course. On each occasion, I managed to extricate myself from the seat and run like blazes from the crackling and smoking aircraft.

It must be realised that, in the Air Force stations in the 1940s, there was no television and few radios. Consequently, there was always a need for entertainment – and anyone who could act, sing or dance, or was generally into music, was in great demand. In the hope that I might continue in the theatre at the end of hostilities, I took every opportunity to volunteer to act and produce at the station theatres. I gathered together singers, dancers, comedians and musicians; my concert party was complete. Sally was our Welsh soprano and sang like a lintie. She was a sergeant WAAF PTI – Physical Training Instructor – a stunning beauty with brown hair, blue eyes and rosy lips. Ah, the lips! I still recall the lips. Let me explain: Sally was the only female in the PTI section. Her team members were all big, strong, muscular young men, mostly over six feet tall. They were a gey lusty lot and found it difficult to keep their eyes away from the attractive sergeant. Sally and I struck up a nice friendship and sat together kissing and cuddling in the station cinema. After walking her home to the WAAF quarters of an evening, I would seek out a wee bit of high ground before enjoying a goodnight embrace and kiss. She was five feet nine inches tall – I was five feet four and a half!

'You're a nice lad, Jimmy,' she explained one night, 'but you know why I allow you to take me home? I wouldn't take any chances with these big monsters in the PTI section. They're too strong for me. But I can handle you, wee Jimmy!' I did not complain. For the record – there wis nae hanky-panky! Sally married her tall marine boyfriend. From my sports meetings prior to joining the RAF, I had collected an array of prizes including five canteens of cutlery. Sally was pleased to receive one of them as a wedding gift.

On my first arrival at Ashbourne, I was promoted to the rank of sergeant. Some of the lads with outstanding exam results were promoted to the first order of commissioned rank – Pilot Officer. My exam results were average and, like the majority, just earned three stripes. Nevertheless, it didn't take me long to learn that a commission could be applied for at any time during RAF service. The pay for a commissioned rank was higher than that of an NCO, and I knew for sure that the catering in the officers' mess was of a higher standard than the food in the sergeants' mess. Wee Jimmy boy decided to apply for a commission. I filled in the application form and waited six months for my interview.

The important day eventually arrived. My 'judge' was Squadron Leader Angus McPherson – a Scot. Hallelujah! He seemed an amiable gentleman – an experienced pilot with many flying hours to his credit, and he wore the DFC and bar. 'Come in, Sergeant. Take off your hat. Sit down.' There was silence for some time while he read over my application.

'OK, Stuart, what makes you think you deserve to be commissioned?' I didn't think it would be appropriate to admit that I was really only interested in more pay and better grub. 'Well, Sir, I feel that I have genuine reasons for wanting a move from the sergeants' mess to the officers' mess. As an instructor I've coped well enough, and I'm still waiting for a posting to an "ops" squadron. My drama club and concert party has been successful here on the station and at the Town Hall. We've raised hundreds of pounds for our RAF benevolent fund. I want to mix with the officers and hold some auditions for new talent. Regarding sport, Sir, I'm the present Mile Champion of the squadron, and I want to seek out some officers for our cross-country team. They spend too much of their free time drinking in the bar.' The Squadron Leader gave me a big smile. 'Thanks, Stuart – we'll let you know.' I got my commission.

In September 1944, I was experiencing a relatively quiet war, still attached to the operational training unit in Derbyshire. I flew with pilots in training and instructed the wireless operators/air gunners. Off duty, I ran for the squadron athletics teams, produced plays and concerts and enjoyed dancing in the village. It was a good time for me. In fact, it was a great life as far as I was concerned, far away from the real action. I wasn't mad keen to be a hero. However, the war was catching up on Jimmy Stuart. Field Marshal Montgomery had a daring plan. It required the American 101st and 82nd Airborne Division to capture the bridges at Eindhoven and Nijmegen respectively and for the British 1st Airborne Division to capture those around the Dutch town of Arnhem. Sadly, the operation was a failure, and many lives were lost. I was not involved in the operation – but, since many air crews were lost, replacement crews were required. They began to arrive at Harwell RAF station in the south of England on 28 September 1944. Leaving from Ashbourne, I joined the crew of a Stirling aircraft piloted by Warrant Officer Dick Draper. The complete crew consisted of a pilot, navigator, bomb-aimer, flight engineer, wireless op/air gunner and a rear gunner. Dick Draper was a young

Englishman from Sussex and one of the most capable captains on the station. He was also the most likeable and modest of men. Happily for me, he was to remain my skipper right until the end of my service. Our crew flew in a Stirling. The front and mid-upper turrets had been removed, leaving a rear turret only. I would have taken the place of the rear gunner in the event of him being injured.

Ten days after I arrived at Harwell, the whole station, including my squadron, moved to Rivenhall in Essex as part of 38 Group. This group provided aircraft (tugs) for towing large wooden and canvas gliders (models Horsa and Hamilcar) and also for carrying parachutists. Until techniques were developed to drop heavy equipment by parachute, the only method available for delivering guns, jeeps and light tanks to a battlefield overseas was by glider. Gliders could be used to transport infantry to the battlefield in concentrated groups, rather than being widely scattered in parachute 'sticks'. The squadron was equipped with converted bomber aircraft – Stirlings, Halifaxes or Albemarles. When not involved with airborne training or operations, we frequently undertook supply-dropping sorties in aid of resistance forces, and also occasional bombing missions. For the next six months, in all weathers, our Stirling–Horsa combinations rehearsed for what we knew would be 'The Big One' – the successful crossing of the Rhine.

At the beginning of March 1945, I was home on leave. One morning, as I was making my way across Carntyne Square, I was warmly greeted by two of my good friends, Mr and Mrs McVean. They were walking with the pram, and signalled to me to speak quietly, as the wee one had just gone to sleep. May Kelt and her soldier lad Duncan had married in March 1943, and Elizabeth arrived on 1 February 1944. They were a very happy couple. On that same leave, one of my best pals, Jimmy Spiers, invited me to be his best man at his wedding later that month. The date was significant.

In March 1945, Adolf Hitler was not enjoying good health. His back was bent, and he was a shadow of his former pomposity. He was swallowing fifty tablets a day. He had been dictator of an empire numbering 300,000,000 people, and boasted that his empire would last 1,000 years. It was crumbling after only twelve years. The Third Reich was nearing its end.

I did not show up on my pal's big day and did not communicate with him. On my return from leave, we were confined to barracks. Telephone calls were not permitted, and the sending of mail was suspended. We speculated. We were eager. The weather had to be right. We waited.

Came the dawn on 24 March 1945, and the greatest airborne operation in history was about to commence. The operation code name was Varsity. Field Marshal Montgomery was informed that Prime Minister Winston Churchill wanted to watch the Allies as they crossed the last barrier on the way to Berlin. Montgomery was not at all pleased, and felt that Mr Churchill would be a nuisance; however, nothing could deter the old warrior. Apparently, Eisenhower was not perturbed and told one of his commanders to make sure there was a good supply of Scotch whisky for 'Winnie'.

Churchill sent this message to the troops: 'British soldiers – it will long be told how, with our Canadian brothers and valiant United States Allies, this superb task was accomplished. Once the river line is pierced and the crust of German resistance is broken, decisive victory in Europe will be near. May God prosper our arms in the noble adventure after our long struggle for King and Country, for dear life and for the freedom of mankind.'

What a morning! Thousands of allied paratroops and airborne troops, packed into a gigantic airborne assault, swarmed across the Rhine ready to swamp the enemy. For the first time, airborne troops flew simultaneously into battle from British and continental bases, pouring across the already breached Rhine in a double stream that seemed endless – 1,500 air transports carrying 40,000 sky-men.

From airfields all over Britain and the continent, streams of tow-planes, gliders and troop-carriers poured for hours after dawn. Captain Dick Draper shook hands with our glider pilot and with each one of his crew. My logbook tells me that we were airborne at 7:10am. I soon watched, above and below me, a bewildering conglomeration of planes, all heading for the Rhine. Long before we reached the English coast, huge American bombers were passing high overhead on bombing missions in support of the ground and airborne attack. Nearing the landing zones, the great American stream on our right surged along parallel with us – and, bunch by bunch, the fighter cover began to whirl overhead and below.

As we edged towards the Rhine, the first Dakotas streaked away below us on the way home. The Rhine, shrouded in smoke for miles, appeared as a silver strand across the fields, and in a few seconds there came a dramatic call from our navigator – 'We're over the river, lads!' The next murderous ten minutes I shall never forget. The air seethed with planes in every direction. Behind us, our Horsa glider, crammed full of eager commandos, went into 'high tow' in readiness for the release. We held unswervingly to the course. There was a last exchange of words on the intercom between our pilot and the glider pilot: 'Good luck'. 'Thanks for the tow – see you soon.' The towrope was cast off, and down went our glider through the flak and away in a steep turn. In our few hectic minutes over the target area, it was possible to look down on a mass of parachutes which made the air look as if a giant thistledown had been destroyed by a gale.

We turned to port when we had released our glider. The sky was criss-crossed with tracer bullets and exploding shells. Dick pushed the control column forward, and our huge Stirling dived. 'That's it, boys – let's go home for lunch.'

I was later to learn that, as we flew home safely to our base, my soldier friend Duncan McVean had been killed on the ground below me. So, for me, on this historic day, certainly the most momentous of my life, I was not aware that my future wife back home in Glasgow had just become a widow. May was hanging out the baby's washing in the back garden when the telegram was handed to her. Duncan would not be coming home. She was 23; Elizabeth was thirteen months old. The war with Germany was to end a few weeks later.

The conflict was nearing its end – and yet, on 7 April, in a freak act of warfare almost overlooked by historians, German ME-109 fighters undertook a massive suicide mission against American bomber formations over Hanover. Having despaired of challenging the Allied armadas by conventional tactics, the Luftwaffe recruited 184 volunteer pilots to ram the Flying Fortresses in mid-air. In that day's action, 133 German ME-109s were lost, with the lives of seventy-seven pilots, for the destruction of twenty-three bombers. At this, its last gasp, the Nazi empire could still summon extraordinary reserves of fanaticism to mark its death throes.

On VE Day, 8 May 1945, I was on leave with my navigator pal, Howard Brown. We mingled with the jubilant crowds in Trafalgar Square and stood in front of Buckingham Palace waving, along with thousands of thankful people, to the King and Queen, and the two princesses and of course Winston Churchill, on the balcony.

On 13 June, our crew made the first of several supply-dropping flights in Stirling aircraft to Norway with much-needed medical supplies. After unloading at the airfield, on this first day, we had some time to spare and were driven by jeep into Oslo. As we drove the fifteen miles from the airport to the city, the villagers and especially the children seemed to be aware of our arrival in their beloved land and were excitedly waving small Norwegian flags and cheering us like conquering heroes.

The city centre seemed extremely busy, and we soon learned the reason for the crowds. King Haakon was due to return to the Royal Palace after five years of forced exile in London. Lined up outside the palace on a downward slope were about 2,000 singers – choirs gathered from all around Norway ready to sing a welcome to their monarch.

Arriving at the back of the mass of people, my rear gunner and I could barely see the palace balcony, so we climbed a tree to get a better view. Two palace guards, noting we were RAF airmen, waved us down from our perch. We gave them some bars of chocolate, which of course they had not seen for years, whereupon they escorted us up to the front of the action. The king appeared, and we listened to beautiful singing from the many assembled choirs.

After the celebrations at the palace, we made our way to the public square. The place was packed with joyful people. Both men and women had donned their national dress, and the colours were magnificent. Flags, banners and garlands were hung from every vantage point, and several bands played at the same time. Beer and champagne were in short supply. No matter. Norway was drunk with happiness. The dancing was hilarious. Paddy and I were hysterical with laughter when we managed to persuade two bonny blonde maids to waltz with us on the cobblestones. They had little English, but we managed to communicate. We missed the jeep arranged to take us back to the airport but managed to hitch a lift after an incredible night.

After VE Day, our crews were engaged in flights to Germany to bring home prisoners-of-war to the UK. I would like to report that those were joyous experiences – and, of course, to a great extent they were. However, my memories of those flights are rather sombre. Our Stirling was packed each time with as many men as we could cram into it. The PoWs were mostly quiet and withdrawn. We were caring towards them, but it wasn't our place to quiz them about their time in captivity. Many of them were pale and emaciated. They all stank to high heaven and – poor souls – had to submit to delousing immediately on landing. My abiding memory of those times was when we approached the white cliffs of Dover. Everybody – but everybody – shed tears.

In October 1945, our crew was posted to RAF station Cairo West, where we were based until we were 'demobbed' in April 1946. We flew from our station in the south of England on a cold, miserable, rainy day and landed eight hours later in

North Africa. We stopped overnight – and the next day, after five hours, we arrived in Cairo West in the Egyptian heat of 90°F. This was going to be a pleasant way to end my service.

During the winter, our crew flew on missions to North Africa, Malta and Italy. I had the opportunity of attending the famous San Carlo Opera House in Naples and heard the great Italian baritone Tito Gobbi. The opera was *La Traviata*. In my time, I've witnessed a few standing ovations, but never one to match that occasion in Naples. The sight and sound of 3,000 excited Italians standing, clapping, smiling and shouting 'Bravo! Bravo!' was a spectacle to behold and remember.

I recall another off-duty day when I was stationed at Cairo West. The great pyramids of Giza had to be visited – and, along with my pilot, Dick, and Paddy our rear gunner, I stood in awe beside the great tombs. The three pyramids of Giza are the greatest of the many pyramids in Egypt and the most famous. The largest pyramid, Khufu (2,600 BC), is 768 feet square and 482 feet high. It covers thirteen acres, took twenty years to build and is constructed of 2,300,000 huge blocks of limestone, fitted together with great accuracy. I knew I might never get another chance: 'Well, lads – how about it? Who's for Khufu?' Dick laughed. 'Jock, you're mad! You'll break your legs. Forget it!' The thought of climbing the world's highest pyramid was too great a temptation, and off I jogged to the base of the edifice. It was a fantastic and exciting experience to 'pech' and sclim up and over the huge blocks. I was surprised to see that each one was about three feet in height, so it was a slow climb. However, in the previous week, I had won the RAF (Egypt) Mile Championship, so I knew I was in peak fitness. 'Mad Jock' reached the summit and waved to his companions far below. On reflection, it was a bit foolhardy. I didn't realise how dangerous it was, and I understand that, because of so many accidents, the climbing of the Great Pyramids is no longer permitted.

One cherished memory of my time in Egypt was on a return flight from the UK. We had been on a week's leave and were just about to land at our base at Cairo West. The date was 13 April 1946, and 139,468 football fans were packed into Glasgow's Hampden Stadium for the Victory International – Scotland versus England. I had been following the match on the radio – and, as the only Scot on board, I had been taking some barracking from the English supporters in the crew. As we landed and taxied along the runway, my earphones seemed to explode with the sound of the famous Hampden Roar. With the score at 0-0 and only sixty seconds to go, Jackie Husband of Partick Thistle took a free kick. It was headed on by my Rangers hero, Deedle Dawdell, Willie Waddell. Celtic's Jimmy Delaney was in the goalmouth and rammed the ball into the English net for a glorious victory! What a GAME! What a happy day!

On Saturday 4 May 1946, I joyfully embarked on a troop ship at Port Said and, in glorious sunny weather, sailed through the Mediterranean and disembarked at Toulon in the south of France at 11pm on Friday 10 May. Then came a long train journey viewing the liberated French countryside and stopping at Calais on the Sunday at 10am. A welcome meal followed before boarding ship again for the last lap and arrival on British soil.

The big hall at London's Olympia was a hive of activity. I received a gratuity of £75 and made my way to the civilian clothing store. Scenes of hysterical laughter ensued as suits, sports jackets, raincoats and hats of varying styles were tried on. After five years of nothing but a service uniform, it was a pantomime to see my mates in pork-pie hats and pinstripe suits!

On Tuesday 14 May at 11:30am, I was officially released from the Royal Air Force, and at 9pm I arrived in my home city of Glasgow and into my mother's loving arms.

Food rationing was still in force. It was great to be home, but I knew that I would miss the fresh fruit that I had become used to – pears, oranges, dates and bananas. Some young children had never tasted these delights. The government even held a banana day, when every child under 18 years of age was presented with one banana!

The kitbag was opened, and all the Egyptian treasures were revealed – Cairo watches, exotic fans, models of the Pyramids and the Sphinx – and two dozen bananas!

7

Bertha Waddell

During my RAF service, I had approached Mr Matthew Forsyth, producer of the Glasgow Citizens' Theatre Company, with a view to employment when I was released. He gave me a warm welcome when I was demobbed in May 1946, and we chatted in his office about my Air Force career. He reckoned that he would be happy to have me in his company, but not right away.

However, he had an idea which would enable me to gain more first-class professional experience. I was to contact Miss Bertha Waddell in Blantyre and explain that he had recommended me. The following day, I found myself in a large house in Blantyre, ten miles from Glasgow, being interviewed for an acting job by two charming middle-aged sisters, Bertha and Jenny Waddell. Bertha asked me if I could sing. I told her I didn't consider myself much of a vocalist. Even so, she made me sing and seemed to think that I would pass muster. She asked me to dance an old-time waltz with her and then perform somersaults in her hallway! Next, I was asked to make some funny faces like a pantomime clown. That wis nae bother to me: playing the fool was one of my hobbies. Acting and miming tests followed, and after about an hour it was time to relax and have a coffee. I then signed a one-year contract with the Bertha Waddell Children's Theatre Company. It was a fully professional company, and actors' Equity rates were honoured.

Bertha Waddell was the daughter of a Glasgow architect. As a child, she had showed singing talent, and Sir Hugh Roberton of Glasgow Orpheus Choir fame suggested that she should compete in the Glasgow Music Festival. She won first prize at the age of 11. In 1928, aged 20, she had the idea of starting a children's theatre presenting plays, fairy stories, music, mime and dancing. Sponsored by the Scottish Committee of the Arts Council, Bertha and her sister had their base at Caldergrove House near Blantyre, Lanarkshire. For ten months of the year, they toured mainly schools, and during the summer break they designed and made costumes and painted props. Bertha wrote plays and dramatised rhymes and songs. Jenny arranged traditional folk airs and played the piano for the group. There were two repertoires – one for the 5–9-year-old group, the other for 9–12-year-olds. All the company members (six in total, three men and three women) were professional adult actors, singers and dancers. Everything was packed into a small van with one member at the wheel and another as passenger. A car followed with the other players. We toured all over Britain – Glasgow, Edinburgh, Manchester, London and Newcastle. My one season with the company seemed to pass very quickly, but I must say it was a great joy to be involved in entertaining the wee ones.

At the start of each performance, Jenny would pop her head through the curtains and sing 'Cuckoo! Cuckoo!' Then she would announce 'Item Number One – The Greedy Boy', or 'Ten Green Bottles' or whatever, then again 'Item Number One'! The children joined in at every opportunity and screamed with glee at the comedy routines. I danced, I sang, I mimed. I acted the young lord, the old Russian gypsy and the clown in the pantomime. My singing improved during the tour.

The company was wound up in its fortieth-anniversary year in 1968. Bertha Waddell's Theatre Company was honoured with giving six command performances at Glamis and Balmoral and one at Buckingham Palace. The first occasion was in 1933 for the Princesses Elizabeth and Margaret.

8

Ginger's Mile

As a boy, my main interest was football. I loved the game, but I'm afraid I was a dead loss in the soccer arena. I was never picked for any of the teams at primary or secondary school. Even at the Boys' Brigade five-a-side games, I was usually the last to be selected.

My interest in running started in 1933 when the CAAC (Carntyne Amateur Athletics Club) was formed. There seemed to be hundreds of young people living in the Carntyne housing scheme at that time, and the formation of an athletic club took off in a big way. During the winter months, we went for cross-country runs (usually three or four miles) on Tuesday and Thursday evenings. Races or inter-club events took place on Saturday afternoons. We were all novices at running, but even at 13 years of age I was capable of keeping up with the older members of the club.

In the early summer of 1934, I entered for the Boys' Brigade local district Athletics Championships and, wearing my CAAC vest and new spiked track-running shoes, I reported to the stadium ready to do battle. I was last in my heat of the 100 yards, was last in my heat of the 220 yards, knocked the bar down at my first attempt at the high jump – and, at throwing the cricket ball, I failed to get past the first round. I was a broken wee lad! I shed my expensive track spikes and put on my sannies. Sergeant Young saw my distress: 'I was just thinking, Ginger, you would probably be more suited to the half-mile race. It's the last event tonight. You ran well in the cross-country training. You've got good stamina.' I appreciated his interest but explained to him that the half-mile was open only to boys aged 16 or over. 'You leave that to me, Ginger! I'll speak to the officer-in-charge. I'm sure I can swing it for you.'

Big Walter was as good as his word. There was an entry of about twenty lads for the race, but most of them were untrained or had started smoking and lacked the necessary puff to stay the distance. Still in my sannies, I was the happy winner of the race and realised from then on that I was destined to be a middle-distance performer.

I went on to win the Glasgow Battalion BB Mile Championship, and I led the CAAC in winning the Scottish Youths' cross-country championship at our first attempt. At the Rangers FC Sports Meeting at Ibrox Park in 1938, I was invited to line up, with others, in an attempt on the 1500 metres world record. Sydney Wooderson, the London athlete and holder of the world mile record, was the star athlete that day. I served as pacemaker; and Wooderson clocked 3 minutes 49 seconds – just one second outside the record.

When I was in the RAF, I won the Cairo Mile Trophy, and in 1946 I won the Scottish five-mile cross-country novice championship from a field of 280 competitors at Pollok Park.

Sadly, the CAAC did not re-form after the war, so I joined Shettleston Harriers. One event which sticks in my mind was a one-mile handicap race at Helenvale Park, Glasgow. I was in good form at the time and started as the 'scratch man' on ten yards, giving allowances (i.e. starts) up to 160 yards, over the four quarter-mile laps. Forty competitors lined up. It is always entertaining for spectators to see the scratch man steadily going through the pack, and more particularly if he is successful. On this occasion, I ploughed my way through the entire field.

The following morning, the *Daily Record* carried a bold headline: STUART WINS BRILLIANT MILE. The reporter then went on to describe the race: 'Diminutive Ginger Stuart of Shettleston Harriers was in great form last night ...'. My mother enquired of me: 'James, what exactly does he mean by "diminutive"?' I replied: 'Mother, he means very, very small'.

'Cheek of him, son!' my mother huffed. 'Imagine calling you small.'

Ah well! A mother's love!

9

The Citz

Matthew Forsyth was as good as his word. At the start of the 1947–8 season at the Citizens' Theatre, I was signed on contract with another young actor by the name of Andrew Buggy. Andrew later changed his name to Andrew Keir. We were both signed up for two years as members of the company and were expected to double as ASMs (assistant stage managers).

I had the satisfaction of working at the 'Citz' until 1957 (latterly as a freelance member) and acting alongside some players who became very successful in television, pantomime and films. Molly Urquhart, Stanley Baxter, Roddy McMillan, Fulton MacKay, John Fraser, Madeleine Christie and John Cairney all appeared at the Citizens' Theatre.

My most abiding memory at the Citz was knowing and working with the great Scottish actor, Duncan Macrae.

In 1943, John Duncan Macrae left teaching to go full-time as a professional actor, at the same time dropping his first name to become known as Duncan Macrae. He trod the boards in Scotland and in London's West End for almost twenty-five years and is arguably the greatest actor Scotland has ever produced. Macrae excelled in all types of productions. He was a first-class dramatic actor, brilliant in comedy roles, and also very successful as a pantomime dame. His films include *Whisky Galore*, *The Kidnappers*, *Tunes of Glory* and *Casino Royale*. He was cast as skipper Para Handy on television in the first series of *The Vital Spark*.

Off stage, he was a gentle, caring, intellectual man. In appearance he was tall, about six feet in height, very lean and muscular. Some critics referred to him as Big Skinnymalinky.

Amazingly enough, John Duncan Macrae's main claim to fame in the eyes of some people was that he sang a daft wee song called 'The Wee Cock Sparra' on BBC television on Hogmanay 1959.

I remember doing a double act with Macrae in a variety bill at the theatre in Kilmarnock. The sketch was titled 'The Mighty Mauler'. Macrae was a champion wrestler matched with an imaginary opponent. I was his trainer and the commentator at the event. Here's the gist of it:

The trainer enters, dressed in a white track suit and sporting a tartan bunnet.

TRAINER: Ladies and gentlemen, it is my proud privilege tonight to introduce to you the most superb specimen of magnificent manhood that the Scottish nation has ever produced! He is a wrestler beyond compare – a man of steel and whipcord – a terror to his opponents. Ladies and gentlemen – let's hear it for Mauler Macrae!

Mauler enters, bows and smiles inanely. He proceeds to go through his pre-fight bending and stretching routine.

TRAINER: Now folks, Mauler is about to unveil to you the body that is a monument to physical fitness. Wonder Boy – let the public see the torso of the century!

The dressing gown is discarded, to loud cheers! The body is revealed – bare chest, yellow long-johns. With incredible contortions, Mauler continues to limber up.

TRAINER: Now folks, you are about to witness the Pride of Polmadie, Mauler Macrae, in action in a grand exhibition bout with the champion of the Gallowgate – Twister McTurk.

The trainer turns round and notes that Mauler is lying flat on his back in some discomfort.

TRAINER: Up now, Mauler – here we go!

MAULER: Ah cannae!

TRAINER: Whit dae ye mean – ye cannae?

TRAINER: Ah shoudny hiv ett thae three fish suppers oan tap o ma tea. Ah think ah've goat cramp in ma kyte!

After a struggle, the trainer gets Mauler to his feet. There's a sound of loud creaking.

TRAINER: Aye, aye, Mauler – a wee bit creaky?

MAULER: That's funny – ah wis well oiled last night.

The fight commences and lasts several minutes. The bell rings. Mauler flops into his chair, lies back and groans.

MAULER: Aw jings! Ah'm jiggert!

TRAINER: Away ye go, man. He huznae touched ye yet!

MAULER: Huznae touched me? Well, there's somebody in here that's goat a helluva spite at me!

Suddenly, Mauler produces a huge wooden mallet from under the mat and knocks out his opponent.

TRAINER: Twister McTurk is out! Mauler Macrae wins with his famous hammer blow. Ladies and gentlemen, another glorious triumph for Scotland's mightiest wrestler!

Mauler raises his arms, then falls flat on his face unconscious!

I suppose every athlete dreams of being a champion. I decided to make a bid for one of the track titles at the Scottish Amateur Athletics Championships, to be held at Hampden Park on a Saturday in June 1948. I'd had a successful cross-country season with Shettleston Harriers, and at the start of the track season had won several mile races; I knew I would be at the peak of my fitness at the beginning of June.

My favourite race was the mile, and I had competed many times over the distance both in scratch and handicap races.

However, the quality of mile runners at that time was very high, and I was pretty sure that I would be pushed even to win a medal. I'd had a little experience over the three miles and the six miles, but not enough to give me confidence at championship level.

'How about the two-mile steeplechase?' I thought. I had never competed in a steeplechase event. It's a race that needs middle-distance pace coupled with a big helping of stamina. My mile racing speed would serve me well, and I had proved my stamina over cross-country races up to ten miles long.

The steeplechase is a gruelling event – eight quarter-mile laps, each containing four three-foot hurdles and one hurdle complete with a water jump. I checked on the possible contenders for this title and reckoned I might have a reasonable chance.

There was, however, one big hurdle to overcome before I lined up on the track. I was of course under contract to the Citz – and matinees took place on Saturday afternoons. Then I discovered that the format for championship programmes was for the steeplechase to be the final event of the afternoon.

The scheduled play at the Citz was Chekhov's *The Cherry Orchard*. I had a part in the play but did not appear in the third act. Yes! It might just be possible to keep myself really busy on that particular Saturday afternoon. The producer gave me permission to be absent from the final curtain call at the end of the play. All that was required now was to arrange for a fast taxi to take me from the stage door in the Gorbals to the stadium at Hampden.

The day arrives. The play begins. I play my part in the first and second acts. I sprint out of the stage door and into the waiting taxi. My minder, brother Ron, is there with a flask of coffee. I shed my stage costume and make-up and don my running gear. The weather is fine, and there are no traffic hold-ups. Hampden hoves into view. I check my watch. We might just make it. Ron pays the taxi-driver, and I jog into the Competitors' Reporting Room and receive my race number for my vest.

'Attention, please! Will all competitors for the steeplechase report to the starting line.'

I had made it!

I had been massaging my legs with olive oil in the taxi, and now had a few seconds to jog up and down to warm up before arriving as the last athlete on the line.

The starter's gun triggered a dozen runners into action. Ron joined my older brother Peter in the stand, and even on my first lap I could hear them shouting for me. At the bell with one lap remaining, I was running neck and neck with Jim C. Ross, a fellow member of Shettleston Harriers. He was older than me, one of Scotland's most graceful runners and a former steeplechase champion. We were still together on the bend after the bell. Up the back straight, we were locked together – and stride for stride we remained so round the final bend and into the home straight. Ron and Peter were losing their voices. The tape came into view, and Wee Jimmy Stuart was the victor by about ten yards.

After the medal ceremony and official photographs, it was back to the 'smell of the greasepaint and the roar of the crowd'!

When the Edinburgh Festival Committee announced early in 1948 that the major drama production that year was to be the great Scottish morality play *The Three Estates*, to say that most people were sceptical would be an understatement. Nevertheless, there were some who felt it was appropriate to produce the archaic Scottish masterpiece at a Scottish-based festival, however limited the appeal.

The following brief summary of the play was given in the programme (published with thanks to the Citizens' Theatre):

Diligence, a herald, summons *The Three Estates* of the realm, namely *Spiritualitie* or Church, *Temporalitie* or Lords and the *Burgesses* or merchants. The poor people of the realm also appear unbidden. *Diligence* makes a little speech to the audience beseeching their silence and craving their patience.

The King of Humanity appears with his courtiers *Wantonness*, *Placebo* and *Solace*. These young men encourage the King to send for *Dame Sensualitie*. They argue and laugh him out of his scruples in the matter of lechery, and the court surrenders to the charms of *Sensualitie* and her handmaidens.

Good Counsel arrives, laments the bad company and bad ways into which *King Humanitie* has fallen and resolves to seek opportunity to influence the King.

Now appear the three vices – *Flatterie*, *Falsehood* and *Deceit* – presented in the manner of the Medieval Theatre as three clowns. They disguise themselves, present themselves to the king and flatter themselves into positions of importance in the realm.

Under the influence of *Sensualitie* and the three vices, the King denies access to *Good Counsel* and causes *Dames Veritie* and *Chastitie* to be cast into the stocks.

At this point, just before the realm is totally ruined and utterly possessed by wickedness, comes *Divine Correction*. The vices flee the land, stealing the King's treasure. Virtue is restored. *Sensualitie*, chased from the King, is received by *Spiritualitie*; and the King, surrounded now by *Veritie*, *Chastitie* and *Good Counsel*, makes promise of amendment and is ordered by *Divine Correction* to summon *The Three Estates* to Parliament to make reforms.

In the first part of the play, Sir David Lindsay is concerned with the moral illness and cure of the individual personified by *King Humanitie*. The second part deals with sickness and restoration of the body politic.

It opens with a farcical interlude between *Poor Man* in search of justice and a fraudulent friar selling pardons and bogus relics. This interlude establishes the two main themes of the second part of the work; namely the oppression of the poor and the corruption of the Church.

Poor Man and *Pardoner* fight and are chased off the scene by *Diligence* to make room for *The Three Estates*, who enter backwards as an outward and visible sign of political retrogression.

When *The Three Estates* are seated, *Divine Correction* bids *Diligence* show that it is their will that every man oppressed makes his complaint. *John the Commonweal* – symbolic figure of the embattled worker and champion of the far weaker, sillier *Poor Man* – makes forcible accusation that *The Three Estates* are led by *Flatterie, Falsehood* and *Deceit.* These three are soon flung into the stocks, and John goes on to make more detailed complaints against the abuses of power by *Spiritualitie.* The needed reforms are agreed by the other two estates in view of their two-to-one majority in the house. *John the Commonweal* is presented with a bright cloak – symbolic of a *Labour Peerage*, while the leaders of *Spiritualitie*, politically, intellectually, morally and financially smashed, are submitted to physical humiliation.

Proceedings are brought to a cheerful close by the public execution of *Falsehood* and *Deceit. Flatterie*, the meanest of the three vices, is allowed to escape, having taken advantage of a moment of indulgence, indeed of negligence, on the part of *Divine Correction.* The escape and apparent negligence are no less allegorical than the rest of the play and are particularly typical of Lindsay's method of conveying his more significant observations by humorous implications rather than explicit and didactic statement.

I have one lovely memory of *The Three Estates*. During the early rehearsals, Duncan Macrae was in his element, clearly enjoying his roles and feeling very much in tune with the producer, Tyrone Guthrie. However, during the second week of rehearsals, he had to contend with an unexpected slap in the face. In one scene, he was delivering a long speech on centre stage. In the background at the bottom of some stairs, a group of townspeople were called upon to shout out with loud protests. One young member of the crowd went over the top and began gesticulating and screaming in an alarming fashion. This upset Macrae – and, just as he was about to appeal to Guthrie to put an end to the overacting of the young man, Guthrie halted the action. Addressing the crowd at the bottom of the stairs, he stretched himself to his full height of six foot three and pointed to the loud-mouthed walk-on: 'You, boy! Yes! You! Stand up!'

A tall, handsome youth with long black hair raised himself from the steps. Guthrie smiled at the lad and instructed him in his impeccable Oxford accent: 'I like what you're doing, dear boy. Don't change a thing. By the way, what's your name?'

The answer came in a firm, clear voice. 'John Cairney, sir.'

Macrae shook his head.

In due course, Guthrie took a keen interest in John Cairney's career. John went on to become successful on stage, on radio, on television and in films. He was an outstanding Hamlet at the Citz, and for ten years toured internationally presenting his own dramatised version of the life of Scotland's Bard, Robert Burns.

I've read about stage understudies taking over from the star of the show, performing very well and thereafter going on to fame and fortune. I remember two occasions when I took over from established actors at the Citizens' Theatre at the last moment (and not even as the understudy). Alas, it did not increase my fame – or fortune.

The Forrigan Reel, by James Bridie, was one of the plays in the Citz repertoire in which Duncan Macrae excelled. During the run of the play, the company was rehearsing for 'the Scottish Play' – *Macbeth*. I think it would be true to say that some performers in the theatre are superstitious types. Some can also tell tall tales. Be that as it may, the production of *Macbeth* on stage seems to have brought about many upsets. Our Glasgow production was not spared.

In September 1949, on the last Friday of *The Forrigan Reel*'s run, Macrae broke his ankle. He was taken to hospital, and after examination it was decided that he was in no condition to perform on the Saturday afternoon and evening. The producer, John Casson (son of Dame Sybil Thorndyke), called a crisis meeting for the Saturday morning at 8:30am. Various different suggestions were bandied about as to how the star's role could be filled. Jimmy Gibson, playing a smaller part, was willing to read the Macrae part, and an assistant manager could read Jimmy Gibson's part. John Casson considered himself for the main part.

I was cast in a non-speaking role and appeared only in the third act. I also shared duties as prompter in the production. We had performed *The Forrigan Reel* once before, and I had been fascinated by Macrae's acting. So much so, that being 'on the book' as prompter for weeks on end, I was very familiar with the script and had (as an exercise for my own benefit) memorised most of the big speeches. Lennox Milne, Gudrun Ure, Laurence Hardy and Lea Ashton all made various suggestions, but John Casson kept swithering.

It was only my second season with the company, and I was still learning the ropes. Even so, I sensed the opportunity. 'Just an idea, Mr Casson,' I volunteered, 'I have most of John's speeches memorised.' Duncan Macrae was always referred to by his first name by members of the company. 'I could manage the part without a script, having been the prompter all these weeks.' There was silence for a wee while. Jimmy Gibson more or less took the decision for John Casson. 'Good idea, James! We'll need to cut a bit off the costume.' Macrae was eight inches taller than me. From 9am until curtain-up at 2:30pm, I rehearsed non-stop with Jimmy Gibson. During that matinee, I only used the script once to read a vital speech; and all went fine in the evening show.

As far as I was concerned, the main drama occurred at the beginning of the third act during the afternoon. In the play, Macrae, as the bizarre Highland dancer, injures his leg and has to hobble on a single crutch. We had altered the costume for me without any problems, but had not rehearsed with the crutch. I was almost due to go on stage when the props person handed me the crutch. I was dangling in mid-air! We screamed for Jimmy McCreadie, the stage carpenter, to bring his saw. With only seconds to go, he lopped eight inches off the crutch, and I stomped into action. A Sunday newspaper had the head-line: 'Steeplechaser Takes the Lead at the Citizens'!'

Roddy McMillan and Fulton Mackay were well-loved members of the Citz, and both became famous on television – Roddy as Para Handy in *The Vital Spark*, and Fulton as the stony-faced warder in *Porridge*. In one of the Christmas pantos, they played the Broker's Men, joking, singing and dancing throughout the show. For whatever reason I can't remember, one Saturday matinee, Fulton did not arrive at the theatre. Once again, the producer called me from the prompt corner and decided that I should partner Roddy.

Using a script would have been a clumsy handicap, so with Roddy's help we gagged our way through the afternoon. I was pleased to see Fulton arrive at teatime.

In my time at the Citz, I experienced many satisfying, dramatic and funny moments. Probably the most exciting episode for me was when I was cast as a wee sailor who was slightly 'under the influence'. The production was the Christmas pantomime of 1951 – *The Happy Ha'p'ny*. Duncan Macrae had moved to the Alhambra, and Stanley Baxter was the Dame.

The final Entire Company scene before the interval was set in Glasgow Central Station. The London train had just arrived, and out poured a very mixed bag of travellers. Those involved included Joan Sims, John Fraser, Andrew Keir, Roddy McMillan, Madeleine Christie – and Stanley Baxter as the star. Various different characters were represented: a very colourful American tourist, sporty types, business people – and Stanley as a flashy, Joan Collins type of film actress.

Each one or group acted out their contribution to the scene and moved off the stage. A loudspeaker announcement blared out and then receded in volume. Jimmy Gibson, as the ticket collector, closed the gate and moved off on the prompt side. There was just the slightest musical hint of 'I Belong to Glasgow' – and a wee sailor, complete with white scarf and small brown attaché case, opened the gate. I had been invited to write my own script. 'Aw, hullo there, Glesga! Ah'm hame!' I lurched to centre stage and stared up at the gods.

There was a cheer and a spontaneous round of applause. 'What a place! Ibrox Park, Lauder's Bar, the Shawfield Dugs, an' the jiggin'!' I did a mock waltz, and a bigger cheer went up. 'Hullo there, Ibrox Park! Hullo there, William Waddell! Get in there boy, on the wing! Give us the old Deedle Dawdell!' At that, I shoogled my legs from side to side in my bell-bottom breeks – and the audience seemed to go hysterical. They clapped, they whistled, they stamped their feet and cheered. At the end of my act, I swayed off-stage, and the curtain descended on the first half of the show.

Each night of the run, the cheering for the wee sailor seemed to get louder. Needless to say, on Saturday nights, with many football supporters in the house, it was a thrill for me to feel the response.

Shortly before his death, I submitted some of my stories to my friend Archie P. Lee, the BBC producer of *The McFlannells*. I had visited him in his home, and we had been reminiscing about the Citizens' Theatre.

He wrote: 'You know Jimmy, I recall one Christmas pantomime when you appeared as a wee sailor. You were in that state never described as drunk, but as "happy". Then, with an expression on your face which was a marvellous picture of admiration and hero worship, you uttered the fervent words "Deedle Dawdell, William Waddell". That is the impression that has lived with me all these years. The brief appearance you made on the stage is one of my unforgettable theatrical memories.'

Willie Waddell was the great Rangers hero at that time. He played on the right wing and will be remembered for his incredibly fast runs down the wing before passing to Willie Thornton. His name has been commemorated in the Ibrox Waddell Suite.

Towards the end of the run of the pantomime, I was informed that Willie himself was 'Out Front' – sitting in the front row of the dress circle. To be sure, the wee sailor gave his act the full treatment that night. Shortly before his death, I had the pleasure of meeting him for the first time and shaking hands with him at a Rangers FC annual general meeting. He seemed frail and used a walking stick. I mentioned the Citizens' Theatre Pantomime of 1951. Alas – so much for hero worship – he had forgotten the night he went to the Citz and witnessed the famous 'Deedle Dawdell Shimmy Shoogle'!

10

Freelance

In 1950, I left the Citizens' Theatre and planned to spread my wings. London attracted me, and I hoped that I might be able to obtain acting engagements in the theatre or in films. However, in the summer of that year, my parents were spending a couple of weeks in Oban. On the final day of their holiday, Mother became unwell and was admitted to Glasgow Royal Infirmary shortly after her return home. She was only in the infirmary for a few short days, and died aged 68 of peritonitis. I have the fondest memories of my mother. She was a gentle, loving and gracious lady. People used to say to her: 'My goodness, Mrs Stuart – none of your boys married yet? You must be too good to them!' They were right. Within three years of my mother's death, all four Stuart brothers were married.

The prospect of London would have to wait. I decided to stay in the family home and support my dad. By this time, my three brothers had all flown the nest.

The Stuart boys were spreading their wings. Jack, the eldest, did well at school. During the war, he was commissioned in the RAF and served as navigator in Mosquito bombers. He chose the hotel business as his career, starting in the Central Hotel in Glasgow. While working as assistant manager at Gleneagles, he met and fell in love with Margaret, the daughter of the Provost of Auchterarder. They were married in 1951 at Auchterarder and moved to Turnberry, where he was now the manager. His work took him to hotels all over Scotland and the north of England. While working in the St Enoch Station Hotel in Glasgow (now demolished), he discovered three floors below ground level and the entrance to a nineteenth-century prison. How eerie it was to walk along the cobbled street and stand at the base of a spiral staircase looking out at the feet of passers-by rushing to Lewis's Department Store.

Like all three of my brothers, Jack was extremely artistic. His pencil drawing of my mother was striking in its classical simplicity. During his retirement, he moved to Kelso, and his artistic focus fell on woodcarving, especially birds. These became so popular that at one point he had to stop supplying the National Trust Shop in Glasgow to concentrate on his local craft fairs, where his carvings were in high demand. He died peacefully in 1997 aged 82 years. Margaret died in 2001 aged 79 years. Their daughter, Gaenor, a lawyer, resides in Edinburgh. Her husband, John Murray, has written his latest book, entitled *Reading the Gaelic Landscape*.

Next to fly the nest was Peter. He was an entirely different proposition from Jack. His horizons spread to the farthest corners of the globe – so, as ship's carpenter, he joined the Merchant Navy. His war was spent as a Petty Officer at the mercy of German submarines. His ship was bombed, but he escaped unhurt. After the war, when not at sea, he worked in the shipyards as a joiner. Although this lacked the romantic appeal of life on the ocean wave, when you are working on what is to be the Royal Yacht there is a certain cachet. This did not dampen Peter's sense of fun. Noticing that my daughter Elizabeth had a packet of sweetie cigarettes that were very realistic, he borrowed them. Waiting until the foreman approached, Peter made a great show of hiding something behind his back. This naturally aroused suspicion. 'Stuart!' yelled the foreman. 'No smoking here.' 'Who, sir, me, sir?' Then, bringing the offending object into view, he proceeded to eat it!

In 1960, Peter emigrated to Canada and found the perfect occupation for himself as an apartments supervisor. His woodworking skills, combined with his charm, made him very popular. True to his career as a carpenter, Peter's artistic abilities were also with wood. His marquetry was beautiful. He married Gladys, a Canadian lass he met at a Burns Supper in Toronto, and it was a happy union. Both died peacefully aged 85 years.

Ron, my younger brother, did well at school. When he left, he worked as an electrician until he was called up in 1944. He was immediately recommended for a commission and was posted to India, where he served as a Captain in the Royal Army Service Corps in Bangalore. On leaving the army, he emigrated to Canada – and, like brother Peter, he met and married a Canadian. Amy died peacefully at home a number of years ago. Ron has one son, John Ronald, married to Heather; two grandchildren and two great-grandchildren. At 90 years of age, Ron is in good health and keeps active as a golfer, woodcarver and sculptor. Inspired by Nicola Benedetti, he bought a violin and tells me he can play some Bach. Do I believe him? Of course I do!

Where was I? Oh, yes – freelance!

In 1951, the Citz recalled me on several occasions, but in 1952 I took the plunge and headed for the bright lights of London. My good friend Archie Duncan from the Citz was making a name for himself in films, and he kindly put me up in his flat. I walked for miles around the offices of theatrical agents and film casting places. When most of my money had run out, I tried selling furniture polish from door to door. Alas – I did not sell one tin! For a few weeks, I worked as a dishwasher at a Lyons restaurant, on the night shift from 10pm until 6am. My spirits rose when I did a tour of London schools with a small Shakespearean company presenting *Julius Caesar* and *A Midsummer Night's Dream*.

Here is a copy of a faded cutting, recalling my one and only West End crit.

First Folio Theatre *Julius Caesar*

On May 17 as part of the Shakespeare Festival, 1952, the Southwark Borough Council presented the First Folio

Theatre in *Julius Caesar* in the George Inn Yard, Southwark. James Stuart as Metellus Cimber swells his small part into an excitement of mighty sound, and his plea to Caesar at the Capitol exceeds the 'Will' scene in interest and anticipation.

When I returned home, I joined the cast of T. M. Watson's popular comedy *Bachelors are Bold*. I had been offered a great part as Willie the milkboy. We toured Scottish towns and cities for three months with enormous success. That wasn't surprising, as Duncan Macae was the star, and he was in magnificent form.

I have a bright yellow-and-red theatre playbill in front of me. It states:

GAIETY THEATRE, KIRKGATE, LEITH
Twice Nightly, Week Commencing Monday, 2 March 1953.
FOR ONE WEEK ONLY
5 New Young Scots Comedians
Jimmy Neil
Jackie Wilson
Don Arol
Andy Stewart
Jimmy Stuart

All five were given equal size in billing space.

At that time, Jimmy Neil was an established performer. For the other four aspiring comics, it was our stand-up variety debut. Andy sang 'Ye Canny Shove Yer Grannie Aff a Bus', incorporating several different impersonations. It went well, and of course he went on to international fame and popularity.

I gave a repeat of the 'Wee Sailor' act from the Citz panto and got a good response. The programme cost tuppence, and the price of a seat in the stalls was two shillings (10p).

In March 1954, I was one of a large cast in Walt Disney's film of *Rob Roy*, starring Richard Todd. It was shot in lovely spring weather in the Trossachs. We enjoyed five-star service in

Jamie with wavy hair, 1945

My parents' wedding day, 1913

Leaning on our
Stirling, 1944:
Howard Brown,
navigator, and me –
the wee one!

Winning the Scottish
two-mile steeplechase
championship for
Shettleston Harriers,
Hampden, 1948

The Three Estates: Sandy Solace (aged 27) and 'fast forward' 65 years!

HOLY SMOKE!

Jamie's Glesca Gospel is top of the Good Book guide

SPREADING THE WORD . . . Jamie Stuart is delighted to have hit the top of the bestsellers' list with his Glasgow version of the Bible

GLASGOW has gone Good Book crazy.

For a vernacular version of the Gospels, in city dialect, has hit the number one slot in the bestsellers' list.

The book, serialised in the Evening Times and published barely six weeks ago, has sold more than 6500 copies. It is already in its third reprint.

And today at his home in Edinburgh Road, Carntyne, author Jamie Stuart said: "I was worried that it might be thought irreverent but

Story: SAM CLARKE

Picture: RAY BELTRAMI

it seems to have attracted a wide readership.

"Ministers have been buying it, as well as people who might not have read the Bible, or not done so for years.

"There have even been orders from Moscow, Norway, South Africa and Denmark."

The Glasgow Gospel, published by the Church of Scotland's publishing arm St Andrew's Press, includes the birth of Jesus, the parables and the Crucifixion.

Mr Stuart, an elder at High Carntyne Church for the past 35 years added: "This has all been very exciting and rewarding.

"The Gospels are the greatest story ever told and I think the new format is lively, entertaining and meaningful."

Mr Stuart, an ex-vacuum cleaner salesman, gents-outfitter, actor and residential child care officer, spent nearly three years preparing the stories.

He said: "A few years ago I wrote A Scots Gospel, which has sold around 10,000 copies and is about to go into its fourth reprint.

"I was approached by minister friends who suggested I do the same for Glasgow."

And he added: "For the first time in my life I was a commissioner at this year's General Assembly, where Hugh Wylie, who wrote the preface to the book, was installed as Moderator.

"After listening to Lord High Commissioner Lord Macfarlane's speech, The Right Rev Wylie presented him with a copy of my book. I was astonished."

Mr Stuart is now working on a new project. "I don't want to say yet what it is but I hope it will be as exciting as the Glasgow Gospel."

The book is available from city bookshops, priced £3.95.

Top of the bestsellers, 1992

Spreading the news, 1992

With the Right Reverend Hugh Wyllie, General Assembly 1992

Queen's Baton-bearer at age 93

the Baillie Nicol Jarvie Hotel. The midges were worrying, but the money was good. It was a ten-week engagement. I was a Highlander one week and a Redcoat the next.

In the summer of that year, I was contracted to top the bill in an English summer show in Swanage on the south coast. The show was called 'Each Evening – An Artistic Summer Entertainment Combining the Cheerfulness of Concert Party with the Sophistication of Modern Revue'. My blurb read as follows: 'Jimmy Stuart – a new young comedian of varied experience, who is already a successful cabaret artist and comes direct from an appearance in the film of *Rob Roy*'. On reflection, I must have passed muster as a seaside entertainer, as I did another season with 'Each Evening' the following year. The show ran for fourteen weeks each summer and was very well attended.

I continued to work as a freelance actor with the Citizens' Theatre, with Dundee Rep and at Perth Theatre. Film and TV parts were in short supply, but I managed to get a fair amount of broadcasting work from the BBC at Queen Margaret Drive.

11

Marriage and a Movie

I know fine that I was always in love with May. As ten-year-olds, we were both members of High Carntyne Church Sunday School and of the Junior Choir. We joined the local harriers – the CAAC (Carntyne Amateur Athletic Club) – when it was formed in 1933. Fund-raising dances were held every Saturday night in the Co-operative Halls in Pettigrew Street, Shettleston, and I remember with pleasure making a sprint for May Kelt when a quickstep was called. She was a great wee birler! In my eyes, she was the bonniest lass in Carntyne, and my heart would beat faster every time I saw her. However, there was no chance for Jimmy Stuart when the last waltz commenced and starry-eyed couples glided round the hall. That privilege always went to a tall, handsome, red-headed lad called Duncan McVean – 'Doakie' to his friends.

Duncan and I were both members of the 162nd Company of the Boys' Brigade and were good pals. He worked, like his father, for the Stephen Mitchell Tobacco Company in Dunlop Street. As a youth, he joined the Territorial Army – and consequently, when war broke out in 1939, he was one of the first to be called up. We must now 'fast forward'.

At 30 years of age, I felt that I should really be thinking of settling down and perhaps even getting married, but at the same time I was loath to part with my independence. I'd had a few brief friendships with girls but never any lasting relationships. May used to come round backstage when I was appearing at the Citizens' Theatre; and, as we lived near each other, we would return together on the bus to Carntyne.

During 1952, I had invited her to several theatre parties. At the beginning of 1953, our trysts seemed to become more frequent. At the end of March, on a Saturday, we attended a most enjoyable Citz Dance at the Central Hotel and returned home in a taxi in the wee sma' oors. I invited May in to have a coffee. My dad had retired to bed. I recall showing her some theatre photographs – probably trying to impress with my ham actor image. Needless to say, I had kissed girls before. As yet, I had not kissed May. Why? Somehow the situation was different with May. Although to my knowledge she had no other attachment, she was a widow with a nine-year-old daughter, and I guess I felt that advances should be sensitive.

Anyway – the night had gone well. May had met many of the well-known personalities. We had danced non-stop, we'd had a glass or two of wine and now were chatting away happily sitting on the sofa. Then I uttered a sentence. It was not in any way premeditated. I just said it. It was intended to be a kind of light conversational sentence. Really, it was a sort of big deal of several staggered sentences.

'You know, May,' I mumbled, 'that was a super night we had tonight – sure was! Great night. Fair enjoyed it. And ...' (there's a pause here – about five seconds) 'yes, you know, May – I want you to understand, pal – I mean this sincerely – I don't consider this friendship of ours to be just a platonic affair.'

'Does that mean we're engaged?' says May. I don't pause for long. I daren't. I swallow. The inclination is to stutter. I speak clearly. 'Sure thing!' I reply. Then it happens – and high time too, we have a cheeper. We got the ring, and on 14 October 1953 we tied the knot in High Carntyne Parish Church, just two minutes from my home in Edinburgh Road.

After the ceremony in the church, my wife and I got into our taxi and were just about to drive away when we heard someone shouting. It was planned that Elizabeth should leave the church with her Aunt Margaret and Uncle Bill. In her excitement, she couldn't find their car. So, what does she do? In a panic, she spots the bridal car and runs towards us. 'Mum! Mum! I can't find Auntie Margaret!' We open the door for her, and the three of us drive away. I've only been married for twenty-five minutes, and already I've a nine-year-old daughter.

In my second year at Swanage, May decided to come down for the last performance, as it fell on the Saturday of Glasgow's September weekend holiday. During the curtain call, I announced to the audience that my new wife had just arrived from Glasgow, having walked the whole way. At the after-show party, you can imagine May's surprise when people kept asking how long it took to walk from Glasgow.

After getting married, I had to reassess my situation. Living at home with my dad, I could cope financially as a freelance actor. It was going to be a different story with a wife and daughter to support. May had stayed with her parents just round the corner from my house, and we decided that she and Elizabeth would move into Edinburgh Road. It was now necessary to supplement my meagre earnings as an actor with some other income.

Seeing an advertisement for vacuum-cleaner salesmen, I decided to have a go. Anyone brave enough was welcomed with open arms into the situation. The basic wage was only £5 per week, so it was vital that sales were made. I was now living in the real world. However, May was working, and I was determined that I was not going to sign on at the Labour Exchange. Even an unemployed actor has his pride!

I soon learned that if I could make a success as a vac salesman, I could easily combine the job with acting opportunities when they came along. The vac firm was not concerned if you left the job for a month or more and then returned to it. As long as their product was sold, they were happy. So, for a period of about four years, I did both jobs, frequently knocking on doors by day and treading the boards or broadcasting in the evening.

Most actors have periods when they are temporarily unemployed. It's called 'resting'. I had an ample share of 'resting'. Was I unhappy? Well, I wasn't full of the joys of spring, but I had a job and I counted my blessings. I loved my wife and daughter, and they loved me. I enjoyed excellent health, and I was always optimistic that there would be good times ahead. I prayed. I sure did pray. Walking along the streets, I would say: 'Lord – you must know that I don't feel madly fulfilled wearing my knuckles away knocking on doors. Please let it be that some day I will do something worthwhile in my life.' I was prepared to be patient.

Now, I have to admit there was no red-carpet ballyhoo for me. However, I did have a part in the film *Rockets Galore* – and the BBC still screen it from time to time. A follow-up to Compton Mackenzie's *Whisky Galore*, it was a gentle comedy about the efforts of a group of Hebridean islanders to thwart the installation of a rocket range on their doorstep. Duncan Macrae played Duncan Ban, one of a quaint assortment of locals whose machinations and exploits held the plot together. The film was made on the lovely island of Barra, off the west coast of Scotland. Most of the cast lived in cottages as guests of the local crofters. Ronnie Corbett (of *The Two Ronnies* fame) and Duncan Macrae spent a lot of time, as a diversion, heaving huge boulders to one another.

I flew to Barra in June 1958 and met up with several of the famous personalities on the set: Jeannie Carson (singing star of many British musicals), Gordon Jackson (the well-loved butler from *Upstairs Downstairs*) and two fine Glasgow actors, Jameson Clark and Jimmy Copeland. I had only one line in the film – but it was a big deal for me, I assure you, and I earned £150. Let me set the scene for my appearance: John Laurie (Fraser from *Dad's Army*) is the captain of the ferry. On arrival at the pier, he mutters: 'Weel then, that wis a gey stormy voyage!' On the bridge as first mate, I reply: 'Aye, it wis thanks to you and God Almighty that we got here at all, Captain!' Laurie sticks out his chest. 'Aye – two ferry guid men!'

Arriving on the beautiful sandy beach which served as the airstrip, I was welcomed by my friend Duncan Macrae. He put me at my ease straight away. 'Jimmy, you'll probably not be called until tomorrow,' he informed me. 'Now then, wee man – d'ye see that bloody big hill behind the hotel? Later on tonight, I want you to run like the clappers to the top and back. We'll give you a marked chuckie to leave at the top to prove that you got there. Jimmy Copeland has a stopwatch to time you. By jings! I'm depending on you, son. You've got to beat the Englishman!' On that note, he was called to meet with the director and left me wondering what on earth he was on about. Jimmy Copeland explained: the unit's favourite entertainment was spectating at the regular hill race between Macrae and Donald Sinden, the very handsome and popular film and stage actor, as they competed with each other to cut down the time it took to run from the Castlebay Hotel to the top of a nearby hill and back. Sinden held the record of one hour and ten minutes. Macrae was a great Scottish nationalist and had a bee in his bunnet from time to time about the English. Macrae seemed scunnered with Sinden's boasting each morning at breakfast about beating him. Although I remembered Donald Sinden as a courteous and friendly gentleman, how could I refuse the challenge?

I decided to forego dinner at 7pm and ordered some scrambled eggs on toast. Two hours later, the Scots contingent waved me off – and, fifty-five minutes later, I sprinted back to the starting line. Macrae was jubilant. With his usual flamboyance, he waited until he spied Donald Sinden entering the hotel lounge before ordering champagne. Then, to complete his satisfaction, he sent for the visitors' book. On the back page of the book, in big capital letters, he wrote:

On this day 23 June 1958 Donald Sinden's record of one hour and ten minutes was smashed by Jimmy Stuart with a time of fifty-five minutes. Scotland Forever!

The incident is mentioned in Donald Sinden's autobiography.

12

Selling, and Social Work

In 1962, my wife and I had a conference. Life was good. We were very happy. Elizabeth was 22 years old and studying to be a teacher; May and I were blessed when we gave her a sister – Fiona – for company in 1958. We were all in good health and praised the Lord for His goodness.

My father had died on 19 December 1959. He was 76 years of age and died peacefully in our home. I know nothing of my dad's early life on the Isle of Mull before he came to Glasgow. This may surprise my family. It doesn't worry me. He was a loving, honest, hard-working husband and a devoted father to his four sons. I loved him dearly.

The time had now come for me to assess my future as an actor-cum-door-to-door-salesman. To make a reasonable income as an actor in Scotland, one has to possess more than just an average talent. May had never been in love with the so-called glamour of the showbiz life, and I had tired of being away from home when a contract was offered outside Glasgow. We both agreed that a nine-to-five job in the city would be a happier occupation. I had no regrets and had learned the skill of acting. It was to prove useful.

A shop manager friend of mine happened to mention to me that his employer was looking for a manager to open a new branch of his television business in Burnbank near Hamilton. Was I interested? 'Yes please,' I said. In due course, I was introduced to Mr Jan Stepek, and he more or less said: 'Let me take you away from all this, Mr Stuart!' Over the next ten years, at different periods, I was the manager of nine of Mr Stepek's shops in Burnbank, Burnside, Hamilton, Motherwell, Bellshill, Airdrie, Uddingston, Lanark and Blantyre. In my time, I had the highest record of sales, so my door-to-door selling had not been in vain.

In 1972, I was tempted to try another job away from the electrical line and answered an advertisement for a job in a high-class furniture store in the centre of Glasgow. The pay offered was most attractive. I got the job and stuck with it for two years, selling three-piece suites, bedroom suites, dining-room items, mirrors and pictures. It certainly was a change of routine, but the pressure remained. One had to graft for business to earn a decent commission on sales. However, the main drawback of the job, for me, was the physical effort demanded of the sales staff. The firm was loath to employ a sufficient number of porters to move the furniture from the store to the delivery vans; consequently, the salesmen were obliged to manhandle their own particular sales. This often meant helping to lift heavy, tall wardrobes or beds – and, as I'm only a wee chap, I wondered how long my poor back would stand the strain.

In the summer of 1974, I was most unhappy with my lot and felt that I really could not continue selling furniture. What did I do? I got down on my knees in my bedroom one night and spoke earnestly to my Maker: 'Lord, I'm sorry to say that I've got to get away from this big shop. Please, if you will, let it be that I can find some other way to earn a living.'

The following week, I was made redundant. I was as happy as Larry. Not so my dear wife: 'What are you going to do? You're 54 years of age. Who's going to employ you?'

I tried to reassure May that I would find something, but she was very worried. As for me, I was honestly relieved to know that I would not be returning to the task of lugging heavy articles of furniture. Then began the chore of writing letters for jobs and visiting offices in the city asking about vacancies. I felt optimistic that my prayers would be answered. I figure there's not much point in praying unless one expects to have a positive response. Then something happened to convince me that my Heavenly Father has an enormous sense of humour.

On the Monday of my fourth 'idle' week, the phone rang. It was the manager of the shop where I had been employed. Surprisingly, business had picked up. Would I please return to the fold? It was good to know that I was wanted, but at the same time my heart sank, thinking about the weight of the wardrobes. 'Oh no! James, this is not happening,' I thought. 'What shall I say?' Feeling that, to an extent, I was in the driving seat, I asked if I could consider the offer and give my answer the next day. The manager was most amenable and said that he would look forward to hearing from me.

May worked as a shorthand typist in a city office. At 5:30pm on that interesting day, she returned home. 'Well, Jamie, any good news today?' I informed her that the shop manager had invited me back to my old job. May's face lit up with joy and relief. 'Oh that's great, Jamie! Wonderful! Great news. When do you start back?'

I had the nerve to swallow a bit and appear to be totally in control of my destiny: 'I said I would think it over until tomorrow.' Well! It would be true to say that my darling wife nearly lost the heid, an nae mistake! 'You said *what*, Jamie Stuart? You said *what*?' Then the tears began – but not for long. My loving partner took command of the situation. 'Are you out of your mind, Jamie? Promise me that you'll ring the shop in the morning and tell them that you'll start right away.' There was no point in arguing. May was right. I went back, albeit with a heavy heart, and slipped back into the old routine.

However! Trust in the Lord! All was not lost. I had applied to Strathclyde Regional Council for a job in social work – and, seven days after restarting my furniture job, I was invited for an interview. I passed the interrogation successfully and was offered a post. I could start immediately. What absolute, utter, tremendous joy! Thanks a million, Lord!

It was with enormous satisfaction that I gave seven days' notice to the shop. There were no hard feelings. They wished me well.

So, in 1974, I joined the Strathclyde Region Social Work Department as an RCCO (Residential Child Care Officer), based initially at Maryhill and then at Larchgrove, Edinburgh Road, in the east end of the city. This appointment was to last until I retired aged 65 and gave me ten years of immense satisfaction and fulfilment. At long last, I was really happy in my job. The routine of social work was entirely to my liking and met my need to do something worthwhile.

When I arrived at the Maryhill unit, on my first day, there were about thirty young lads in residence, ranging in age from about nine to 16 years old. Their problems were varied: some had been bullied by their parents, some had been abused, and others had been engaged in criminal acts such as housebreaking, shoplifting, mugging and car theft. Drink, drugs and glue-sniffing were big problems. The 1970s saw the emergence of the new profession of social work. As society became more complex, but also more compassionate, various programmes were developed to help those in need. There was a rapid expansion in job opportunities; and these attracted mature people who could bring understanding as well as practical life experience to the job.

Scotland's radical Children's Hearing system, which sees young people in trouble as being in need of help, guidance, education and support, appealed to me very much. I saw the opportunity to work for welfare rather than punishment. Assessment centres had been established to replace remand homes – places aiming to determine not only why the youngsters were in trouble but also how they could be helped. The Children's Panel would order a boy or girl to attend or stay in an assessment centre for three weeks, or for longer if more investigation or support was necessary.

I have before me a profile of myself written by my senior social worker in 1975:

The boys who came to the centre where Jimmy Stuart began his career were upset, confused and suspicious of adults. And what about 'auld Jimmy'? – what did he know? Well, he certainly knew the importance of fun and laughter. He was someone who would take an interest in you. Make sure you were clean and tidy and well fed. Riotous laughter could be heard as Jimmy embarked on an impromptu song-and-dance routine or a joke-telling session. Indeed, colleagues would often remark at the end of an evening: 'The boys were fine, but see that man Stuart!' His old skills as an actor and salesman were put to good use. Some of the boys had tragic backgrounds with little or no family support. Bumped from children's home to foster home and on a constant not-so-merry-go-round, their behaviour deteriorated until they ended up stuck in an assessment centre with nowhere to go and facing a bleak future.

Jimmy had a particular interest in these boys, and one summer he organised a week's holiday for them in Blackpool during the Glasgow Fair. He persuaded the manager of the Pleasure Beach to part with free vouchers for the carnival roundabouts, and the lads had a ball. Of course, no holiday would be complete without a visit to a posh hotel. How could Jimmy pull this off? Well, he did. That was the easy bit – the hard part would be ensuring that the boys behaved, especially when it was discovered they could use the swimming pool. Jimmy remembered the story that the English comedienne Dora Bryan told about her naughty small son 'performing' from the high diving board! He gathered his team around him and, with a serious face, explained that this was a modern hotel with all the latest technology, including a 'pee-meter' which set off a loud alarm if there were any 'accidents' in the pool. These lads were all street-wise, but surprisingly enough they actually believed Jimmy's warning and obediently visited the facilities before entering the pool.

It's never too late to go back to school. Jimmy was determined to make a career as a social worker, wanting to be better at helping those in need. At long last, attending night school, he passed his Higher grade English exams and then began a course of study which would last almost three years to gain the certificate in Social Studies – one of the oldest successful students in the United Kingdom.

One of the boys I had to deal with was Charlie. Charlie was 15 years of age and six feet tall. He had the mental development of a ten-year-old and had to be treated like a child and humoured a lot when he got out of hand. Referred to the police by his parents, he was being assessed because of his habit of shoplifting and bag-snatching. Most of the time, he was well-behaved, accepted discipline and giggled a lot. I had a good relationship with big Charlie – and, when he was depressed, I would take him for a walk on the football pitch and recite daft poems or sing 'The Wee Cock Sparra'. He seemed to like me. As events transpired, I was thankful that we could communicate.

The drama happened on a Saturday morning. Most of the boys had been granted weekend leave. Charlie's leave had been denied because of unruly behaviour. To say that Charlie was unhappy would be an understatement. He was bitterly angry – left the dormitory, and quite slowly and deliberately began to hurl bricks at the school windows. He smashed about thirty of them. Taking my life in my hands, I ventured into the yard to confront our rebel. Seeing me coming, he picked up a very heavy rusty chain, began swinging it wildly and warned me not to come near. In the corridor, the staff held their breath. Like a brave movie star, I walk slowly forward. 'Don't come near, auld Jimmy – ah'll hit ye!' I get nearer and nearer. The nasty chain continues to swish ominously. 'Jimmy – ah tellt ye,' says Charlie. I now move straight into the danger zone. The chain strikes my shoulder (it doesn't hurt me in the slightest). I scream out in agony – and, like the awful corny actor I am, begin to bawl and cry like a baby. Charlie drops the chain, puts his arms round my shoulder and begins to weep in company with me. Sobbing pathetically together, we proceed to the dormitory, have a Coca-Cola and a game of table tennis.

13

A Seed is Sown

In September 1981, I paid a visit to the Edinburgh International Festival and witnessed an acclaimed one-man dramatic presentation by Alec McCowen. The English West End actor had memorised the whole of Mark's Gospel from the King James Version of the Bible. His performance was sensational. He played to packed houses and received standing ovations. This presentation by McCowen had a significant impact on my life and triggered off a remarkable sequence of events which, in my wildest dreams, I could never have imagined happening to me.

Returning home in the train between Waverley Station and Queen Street, my wee head was bursting with a plan. I felt the urge to emulate McCowen's feat in some way. I believe that, if we have a worthwhile talent, then we should use it for personal fulfilment and also, hopefully, to please or inspire other people.

'Right then, James,' says I to myself, 'you're inspired by McCowen. What can you do about it?' McCowen had recounted the Gospel in the English language. I could tell the story in the guid Scots tongue! I had a fair idea it had never been done before in an acting format – and, from my experience as a professional actor in the Glasgow Citizens' Theatre, I had acquired a good working knowledge of the Scots language. I remembered that I had a copy of *The Four Gospels in Braid Scots* written by the Reverend William Wye Smith and published way back in 1901. I contacted the publishers and was given permission to adapt the work for dramatic presentation. This did not work out very well, and I decided to go it alone.

Over a period of two years, I combined the four gospels of Matthew, Mark, Luke and John into one single narrative, had all the handwritten pages typed out and memorised the script. My own minister at High Carntyne Church, the Reverend James Martin, invited me to present a short passage of the work during a Sunday morning service in our kirk. It seemed to meet with approval. I was encouraged.

In the autumn of 1982, I journeyed to Edinburgh with a view to speaking to the Church of Scotland Director of the Netherbow Arts Centre. Some years earlier, I had broadcast with the Reverend James Dey at the BBC in Glasgow, and I reckoned that he might give me some guidance. The Netherbow is annexed to John Knox House in the cobbled High Street. On arrival, I was welcomed by a tall, bearded young man who informed me that Mr Dey was on holiday. 'Oh right,' I said. 'Many thanks, I'll call again.' I turned to head for the door. I expect the young man was curious. He certainly was very friendly. 'Can I be of any help?' he volunteered. That meeting is fixed in my memory. My immediate reaction was a feeling of embarrassment. Was I prepared to pour out my ideas to a total stranger and risk a dent to my enthusiasm?

'I wanted to ask Mr Dey for some advice about some writing,' I answered. 'I'm an elder in High Carntyne Church in Glasgow. I used to do a bit of acting, and I thought of presenting the gospel story in dramatic form – in the guid Scots tongue!' The good Lord sure works in wonderful and unexpected ways. The young man was Dr Donald Smith, and at that time he was the Assistant Director at the Netherbow. 'Tell me more,' he said. 'It might interest you to know that I took my doctorate in the Scots language at Edinburgh University. It seems like a great idea. Why don't I take you to our wee theatre downstairs? Can I hear some of the piece?'

We made our way down to the theatre, and I presented the Good Samaritan and the Prodigal Son. From that moment, my project really took off. The Reverend James Dey moved on some months later, and Donald Smith took control of the

Netherbow. He suggested that I call my effort *A Scots Gospel*, and offered to help me. Thereafter, I made several monthly visits to Edinburgh, and Donald edited the entire work.

Prior to seeing Alec McCowen in 1981, I had never really done any serious writing, so this was an exciting and fulfilling experience for me. May was not at all sure that there was any real worth in what I was trying to do. Nonetheless, she supported me in every possible way and wished me well.

When May and I married in 1953, we were both smokers. At 40 years of age, I stopped and smugly felt that everyone else in the world should do the same. May was not a heavy smoker, and I did all in my power to persuade her to stop. She knew that cigarettes were bad news but felt powerless to give them up. She even tried help from a hypnotist, with no success.

Early in 1981, May had her first heart attack. Her doctor advised her to give up smoking, saying that it would not guarantee that she would not have another heart attack – but, if she did not stop there and then, she would die. My dear wife took the advice and stopped smoking.

In January 1983, she had another heart attack. It hurts me to hear any criticism of the staff at Glasgow's Royal Infirmary. The doctors and nurses were magnificent in their kindness and care. May died peacefully aged 61 on the evening of 9 February 1983. We had enjoyed thirty years of loyal happy union.

I cannot find the words to describe my feelings when May went out of my life. I did a lot of praying, and I know my prayers were answered. God promises strength and comfort to believers. It now seemed to me that writing was going to be my salvation.

14

The Marathon

During the 1970s, there arose a big interest in marathon running which seemed to climax around 1980. In the USA, thousands of athletes and untrained optimists all wanted to experience the great ego trip and casually boast of winning a marathon medal. Everyone who completed the distance received a medal.

There is a kind of fascination about the marathon – the classic running event of 26 miles and 385 yards. It's recognised as a test of great endurance. The name stems from the legend of a battle near the Greek town of Marathon in 490 BC. The Athenians were victorious over the Persian army; and a Greek soldier named Pheidippides was directed to take the news of the success to Athens. He ran the twenty-two miles from the battlefield, arrived in Athens, shouted 'Rejoice, we conquer!' and, sadly, fell down and died.

Chris Brasher, the English athlete and former Olympic steeplechase champion, organised the first London Marathon in 1981. I was caught up in all the *brouhaha* – and, in 1982 (at 61 years of age), I entered and completed the London Marathon. Later the same year, I finished the first Glasgow Marathon with my best time of three hours and fifty-nine minutes. It's exhilarating to be involved in the excitement and camaraderie of the event; and I was pleased to raise some money for Christian Aid and Save the Children.

Like most competitors in the marathon, I 'hit the wall'. Marathon runners have long recognised that there comes a point in the later stages of the race, usually between eighteen and twenty-three miles, when running suddenly becomes very much harder. Suddenly, without warning, the runner is dragged down to a much slower pace, despite increased effort. Weak legs, acute muscle discomfort and fatigue, together with severe doubts about even completing the distance, accompany the change. The sensation is commonly known as 'hitting the wall', because that is what it feels like.

After approximately eighteen miles of hard running, the muscles have used up their chief energy-providing source, glycogen (which is stored carbohydrate in the form of sugar), and a chain reaction sets in as new stocks of fuel are urgently sought by the muscles. The body switches to using fat for fuel. This, although readily available, is a less efficient alternative. I 'hit the wall' twice but managed to run through it and finished in one piece, tired but elated. I could have cried with joy – and, later on, I did in fact shed tears. In emotional circumstances, I don't think it's surprising that grown men cry. God gave us the ability to bring on helpful tears when they are required. What sports follower will ever forget the amazing sight of the former Rangers and England football star, Paul Gascoigne, weeping buckets on the field when England were defeated during the 1990 World Cup? Towards the end of his running career, Steve Ovett and his fellow Olympian, Sebastian Coe, were set up together in a very emotional mile race duel. The race organisers had misled Ovett about the conditions of the event; and, after the race, in a television interview he wept uncontrollably.

In September 1982, I was in church one Sunday morning sitting quietly. The minister was reading the intimations when I suddenly heard my name being mentioned. 'And now, friends, we have a surprise for our elder, James Stuart. After his success in the London Marathon earlier this year and the Glasgow Marathon last week, I can reveal that Christian Aid has benefited from his efforts.' I was signalled to come forward. 'James – we would like you to accept this trophy to mark your achievements.'

I collected my award and, as I returned to my seat, unashamedly enjoyed a nice wee bubble.

15

A Scots Gospel

In the autumn of 1983, I found solace from my grief at losing May when I joined my minister, the Reverend James Martin, and his group on a visit to the Holy Land. It was an unforgettable experience.

On the first day, our coach took us to Bethlehem. Leaving Jerusalem, we passed places which were to become landmarks during our stay in the area: Gethsemane, Lion's Gate and St Andrew's Church. We visited the Shepherds' Fields, where it is reckoned that the shepherds saw the angel telling them of Christ's birth. There has been a church on this site since the fourth century AD.

Arriving at the Church of the Nativity in Manger Square right in the heart of Bethlehem, we entered by the door where every person must bend the head to view the birthplace of our Lord.

Returning to Jerusalem, we headed for St Stephen's Gate to begin our first visit to the Old City. The walls of the city have been rebuilt sixteen times.

We travelled to the lowest spot on the surface of the earth, and some of us floated in the buoyant waters of the Dead Sea, where the salt content is around 26 per cent. Our minister lay on his back in six feet of water and read a newspaper.

A few miles from the Dead Sea, we saw the spectacular Rock of Masada, which is 1,000 feet high, and I remembered reading about Herod's great palace built on top of the mountain. In AD 70, 980 Jews escaped from the Romans in Jerusalem and fled to the safety of Masada. The Romans followed, determined to capture the stronghold. For three years, as many as 10,000 Roman soldiers camped at the base of the mountain. They built a ramp and eventually reached the summit of Masada. Breaking through the barricades, they were met with a great silence, for the Jews had chosen suicide rather than capture. Most visitors make the 1,000-foot ascent to the summit by cable car. Being in training for another marathon, I spotted the snaking path, and jogged to the summit and back. I was given a certificate and T-shirt from Mr Martin – 'Conqueror of Masada'.

I have a cherished memory of the time when we arrived in Tiberias. On a lovely, still, cool evening, just as the sun was setting, I gave my first public reading of *A Scots Gospel* to our group. The reading took place on the roof garden of the Church of Scotland Centre overlooking the Sea of Galilee.

Although I was presenting the Gospel, I felt that our group was involved in the story-telling. It was a joyful feeling. Somehow, on that night, it seemed to me that everyone in the entire world was happy and at peace with their neighbours.

It was refreshing indeed to take part in the pilgrimage/holiday to the Holy Land, as I endeavoured to come to terms with life without May. Sadly, my wee family suffered another crushing blow on my return in September.

Weir Pumps of Cathcart had employed my son-in-law Iain for all his working life. He married my daughter Elizabeth in 1968; and their only child, Kirsty, was born in 1976. Although Iain had leukaemia for most of his adult life, it was not until 1983 that the condition became acute. His health deteriorated during the summer of 1983, and he died in the Victoria Infirmary on 11 October 1983, aged only 41.

Iain Harvie was a kind, loving husband and father. He was a small man – like myself – just five feet four inches tall, but his stature didn't affect his abilities in so many directions. He was a first-class engineer, mechanic and joiner. It was always his ambition to sail his own boat, and he worked hard to make this dream come true. He and Elizabeth owned their own folkboat – named *Polka* – and berthed it first at Rosneath and then at Gourock. Mum, dad and Kirsty enjoyed several happy summers sailing to Rothesay, Ardentinny and Tarbet.

In 1985, Donald Smith arranged a tour of churches, schools, theatres and prisons throughout Scotland for me to give my one-man dramatic presentation of *A Scots Gospel*. I had memorised everything but usually placed the manuscript on a lectern in case of emergency. The presentation was in two parts, each fifty minutes long, with a twenty-minute interval.

In the autumn of 1985, my friend the Reverend Jim Martin (no relation to my own minister), formerly of Kilsyth Congregational Church and now an international evangelist, contacted his brother the Reverend Robert Martin in Canada to set up a tour of churches in northern Ontario. Rob Martin put me up in his lovely country home in Vankleek Hill and arranged everything. My first appearance was a safe one, to the ladies of the Women's Guild. Bless the ladies. In Canada, as in Scotland, they are the backbone of the Church. All went well. Performances were given in Presbyterian churches in Hawkesbury, Vankleek Hill, Lancaster, Howick, Kempville, Finch and Ottawa.

During the General Assembly of the Church of Scotland in 1985, the Church and Nation Committee said that our people should give more thought to the Scots language. I'm pleased to report that the Scots-Canadians I met on my tour had a great love of their Scottish heritage and culture. The response by Scots, Canadians and others to the story of Jesus told in the Scots language was similar to the reactions I had experienced in Scotland. At the receptions after the performances, I met Scots from Aberdeen, Ayr, Kilmarnock, Edinburgh and Glasgow. Some of them had emigrated a long time ago and had never returned to visit the land of their birth. They were filled with emotion to hear the familiar Bible stories told in their ain guid Scots tongue. In my travels, one lady was fair chuffed to hear me declare: 'Let us eat and be blythe, for ma son wis deid an cam back tae life once mair: he has been tint an is fund'. She

had memorised the wording on an old sundial near her home:
'Tak tent o time, ere time be tint (*lost*)'.

16

Paper Boy

I have usually been fortunate with the regularity of my morning newspaper deliveries. However, in December 1988, my boy 'retired', and my newsagent was having extreme difficulty finding a youngster for the Edinburgh Road run. After complaining about not getting my *Herald* delivered, I jokingly said to the lady manager that I felt like offering myself for the job. She was on the receiving end of a lot of hassle from the customers. 'Mr Stuart, I hope you're not kidding! That would be great! When can you start?' On an impulse, I told her that I'd be at the shop at 6am the following day.

I left the shop in a daze. My only worry now was how my schoolteacher daughters would react to my going back to work aged 68. When my younger daughter Fiona arrived home from work, I told her of my morning job. 'Ha ha! Very funny, Dad!' she laughed. Then it dawned on her that her eccentric old dad was serious. 'My goodness, the neighbours will think you're doing it for the money.' The pay was £9 per week!

As promised, I reported on time the next day and continued the job for six months. I set my alarm for 5:30am each day and got stuck into the idea of being a paper boy once again. As a boy, I had delivered papers on the same route for four years, so I was turning back the clock just over fifty years. What an incredible experience it was. Thomas Carlyle wrote: 'Work is the grand cure for all the maladies and miseries that ever beset mankind.' He was so right. However, as a retired person, I was not at all unhappy; on the contrary, I was living life to the full, and here was a golden opportunity to test my discipline at early rising. The shop employed another four paper boys; I mixed in with them and was accepted as one of the team.

In December and January, we had some very heavy snow, and I can remember at least two mornings when the hailstones seemed to batter through my balaclava like pellets from an air-gun. I worked out the shortest routes from door to door and vaulted over fences when the opportunity arose. Most of the time I jogged, and the feeling of euphoria when I pushed the last *Herald* or *Record* through a letterbox was a lovely experience. Breakfast was enjoyable, as I felt that I had earned it.

When the spring arrived, it was a joyous time to be bouncing up and down paths with my bag full of world and local news: good news, bad news, war, peace, scandal, sport, politics, personalities, TV programmes, forecasts, fashion, agony columns and articles for sale – all waiting to be digested by my readers. March and April were my favourite months. In the early morning, there was little traffic. The smell of springtime at 6am is enchanting. The birds seem to sing at their sweetest, the buds in the trees and shrubs are pulsating with life, and of course the snowdrops and daffodils are wondrous to behold.

At the end of May, a wee lassie wanted the job. I hung up my bag. I was sorry to leave.

17

Author

After I had returned home from Canada, the Church of Scotland Pathway Productions Unit made an audio cassette of my theatrical performance. The next development floored me completely. Donald Smith telephoned to inform me that Saint Andrew Press, the publishing house of the Church of Scotland, wanted to publish *A Scots Gospel*. 'Come on, Donald!' I said. 'You're joking! Publication? This is Jimmy Stuart you're talking to – repeated his second year at Whitehill School – sold vacuum cleaners door-to-door for four years! Are you serious, Donald? Will I be called an author?'

My wife May was the only person who ever called me Jamie. I had an idea. How could I make her a part of this new venture? *A Scots Gospel* by Jamie Stuart was launched in the Netherbow Arts Centre in Edinburgh on Tuesday 19 November 1985. We received coverage on television, on radio and in the press. The *Glasgow Herald* reported: 'The well-known story of Jesus of Nazareth is re-enacted in the gutsy vernacular of the Scots tongue – delightful and dramatic – it demands to be aired publicly, or read aloud around the family fire.'

Dr Donald Smith wrote the following introduction:

Taken along with the development of the Glasgow Citizens' Theatre, the astonishing growth of the Scottish Community Drama Association and the foundation of the Edinburgh International Festival, the Edinburgh Gateway's twenty-one years of active existence are evidence not just of the renaissance in Scottish Theatre, but of a new alliance between church and theatre which was sealed by the triumphant production of Sir David Lindsay's sixteenth-century morality play *Ane Satyre of the Three Estaits* at the Edinburgh Festival in 1948. Directed by Tyrone Guthrie, the play was performed in the Church of Scotland Assembly Hall by a distinguished Scottish cast, which included the author of *A Scots Gospel*. This dramatisation of the Gospel story in colloquial Scots, conceived by a Scots actor, will certainly be enjoyed by audiences in churches and theatres alike.

The John Knox Press of Atlanta in the USA published an American edition of *A Scots Gospel* with an all-blue tartan cover and with this introduction: 'For all who find roots or romance in Scotland, who delight in the sound of a broad Scots burr and the skirl of the pipes, who rejoice in the soft beauty of a tartan and the imposing dignity of a kilted Highlander. May your hearts be lifted up by hearing again, in this new way, the old, old story of the life of our Lord among us.'

In the wake of *A Scots Gospel*, a number of Glasgow ministers suggested to me that I should consider writing the Gospel stories in the Glasgow vernacular. I hesitated. Many people love the pithy, pungent patois of Glaswegians, while many others have little regard for it. My good friend the Reverend John Campbell, the Church of Scotland Advisor on Mission and Evangelism, encouraged me. 'Jamie, I'll tell you something,' he said. 'From time to time, I pay a visit to the Barras on a Saturday morning with the express intention of listening to the Glasgow Patter. It's a real joy. Why shouldn't the greatest story ever told be presented in the language of the people? It's never been done before. Jesus must have conversed in the ordinary language of the people.'

During 1991, John Campbell called in to my home in Carntyne frequently and guided me in the intricate task of translating the Gospels into accessible and meaningful Glasgow-speak.

Every big city has unpleasant slang terms of communication, so it was important to avoid colloquial language with unacceptable words and usages.

The launch of *The Glasgow Gospel* was scheduled for 16 April 1992 in the Church of Scotland bookshop in Buchanan Street, Glasgow. On the previous Monday, the Church of Scotland issued a publicity release to Associated Press. It went round the world on 'the wire'. On the Tuesday, the phone never stopped ringing. The BBC, ITV, Radio Scotland, Radio Clyde, Radio Wales, Radio Belfast and Toronto Radio all interviewed me by telephone. From the USA, Washington DC Radio wanted to speak with 'Mr Stoo-art'. The interview was broadcast coast to coast. Imagine the surprise of one of my friends, who was cruising on the *Canberra*, when she heard my voice coming from the radio. On the Wednesday morning, I was awakened at 6am by the phone ringing. It was a request for an interview with Melbourne Radio. Meanwhile, in Glasgow, Radio Clyde was broadcasting an advertisement for the *Glasgow Evening Times*, which was serialising chapters from the book – two whole centre-page spreads, Monday to Friday – in colour.

In the Saint Andrew Press office in Edinburgh, they were getting some strange requests – a local kiltmaker's order had to include six copies of *The Glasgow Gospel* for a customer in the USA. Also, on Easter Sunday, the lunchtime ITN news carried a feature on the Pope's address, a message from the Archbishop of Canterbury – and Jamie Stuart with *The Glasgow Gospel*.

On the Thursday, Lesley Duncan of the *Glasgow Herald* phoned me to request a copy of the book for reviewing on the Saturday. She couldn't find a copy in any of the shops, as the first edition of 3,000 copies had sold out within hours. I took a copy to the *Herald* offices. Lesley Duncan interviewed me. In her review, she wrote: 'Had I two minutes to spare? Of course I had. That is how I found myself listening, a transfixed audience of one, to the Parable of the Prodigal Son rendered in Glasgow patois. The reader was Jamie Stuart, 71-year-old elder of High

Carntyne Church, whose paperback, *The Glasgow Gospel*, has propelled him into unexpected national celebrity this week.'

With all the *brouhaha* surrounding the publication of *The Glasgow Gospel*, and seeing the wee book go to number one in the Scottish bestsellers' list, I thought it might be a good idea to exploit the interest and try to raise some money for a good cause. I asked the director of Save the Children if she would approve of the Church of Scotland making a video film of *The Glasgow Gospel*, with profits going to the Save the Children charity. She was delighted to consent.

Laurence Wareing was in charge of Pathway Productions, the Kirk's video unit in Edinburgh. We knew each other well, as he had produced my audio cassettes of *A Scots Gospel* and *The Glasgow Gospel*. I explained my idea to him over the phone, and he came to my home to discuss the feasibility of filming the book. Laurence knew little about locations in Glasgow. 'Where would we make it, Jamie?' he asked. 'No trouble at all in that respect, Laurence,' I replied. 'We'll use Sauchiehall Street, Buchanan Street, Argyle Street, George Square, the City Chambers, the Royal Concert Hall, the People's Palace, the Museum of Transport, the Cathedral, Botanic Gardens – will I go on?' 'No, Mr Attenborough, stop there! How do we get permission to film in these places?' I reminded him that Glasgow was 'the friendly city' and that it was unlikely that we would find any difficulty with permits for shooting. Laurence was warming to the potential. 'All right, Sir Jamie, who's going to star in this epic production?' I was ready for this. 'Laurence, dear sir, this the easiest part of my whole idea. As an old has-been actor, I am still in touch with personalities in the entertainment circle' – and I reeled off a list of famous names. Laurence was impressed. 'One wee point, Jamie: how do we know these folk are going to work without any fee?' 'No headache here,' I assured him. 'If they're not prepared to give their time to Save the Children for free, then they don't take part.' There was little doubt in my mind that the aforementioned artists would be willing to co-operate if they were available.

I had the feeling that, when Laurence came to see me that day in my house in Carntyne, he really intended to be polite, to listen to me and to tell me that my idea was too ambitious. As it turned out, we drank a lot of coffee and talked for three hours. The month was August. In order to set up the administration, approach the cast and plan to have the video on sale in the shops in November to catch the Christmas market, we realised we would only have two weeks to do the actual filming. It was going to be a tight schedule, and the weather clerk would have to be kind to us. Alison Fleming (of Pathway Productions) started telephoning our chosen people. My good friend Jimmy Black, author, poet and great authority on Glasgow, volunteered to take Laurence and his film crew on a reconnaissance of the city; and some very interesting locations were identified. Permission was granted for all location filming, and Stewart Black was commissioned to compose original theme music. Filming commenced on 6 October and was completed by 30 October. We were blessed with dry weather, and all went well. Jimmy Black presented the Nativity Story from the Queen Mother's Hospital. The youngest member of the company was Amanda – just twenty-four hours old – who played the part of baby Jesus. She was brilliant and took direction without a murmur.

Andy Cameron delivered the parable of the Prodigal Son from Central Station, and Johnny Beattie read Peter's Denial from the Italian Centre. Laurence didn't allow me to choose my own scenes, but I was not surprised to be cast as Zacchaeus. There is only one tree in Argyle Street. It's been there a long time and is regarded as a 'listed tree'. I volunteered to sclim up the tree; alas, the director would not allow it!

Alex McAvoy's depiction of the crucifixion, filmed in the Necropolis, was quiet and sensitive, while Mary Marquis's telling of the resurrection scene, set in the Botanic Gardens, was incredibly moving. To complete the cast, I invited my elder daughter Elizabeth to take part, and also the former director of the Citizens' Theatre, Lea Ashton. Last but not least, my friend the Reverend Jack Lamb presented the chapter on John the Baptist. Jack is now working as the minister at Townsend Road Presbyterian Church in Belfast, between the Shankill Road and the Falls Road. I joined two busloads of supporters from Stirling attending his induction there.

One of the first people I invited to appear in the video was my good friend Alastair McDonald, the popular Scots folk singer. It was an inspired choice! Alastair had become a Christian more than a decade earlier, since when he has become a driving force in evangelism. Laurence Wareing wanted Alastair to be in the market place casting out the money-changers and pigeon-dealers. There was never any doubt about the most suitable location: Glasgow Barrowland – the Barras!

We set up one Sunday morning during the hustle and bustle of the market. Alastair was in dramatic mood: 'When Jesus went intae the Temple, he wis furious at whit he saw gaun oan. Barras everywhere – wheelin an dealin! At wance he heaved ower the tables o the money-chyngers, an upset the stools o the pigeon-dealers, cryin oot: "God said this Temple is for prayer an worship. You lot hiv turned it inty a den o cheats!"'

Laurence finished the shot with Alastair but then panned the camera to the side, where a young busker was playing his guitar and singing Bob Dylan's *Knocking on Heaven's Door*. Did he get an answer to his knocking? This is Alastair's account of what happened on that Sunday and of a certain sequel:

On the Sunday morning Laurence, Jamie and I met in the Barrowland office prior to going out on the shoot. It was agreed that a word of prayer would be in order. We prayed.

Months later, my wife and I were attending Spring Harvest, a Christian festival held in Ayr, when a young man approached me and said: 'Hi, you and I appeared in a video together!' His face did appear to be kind of familiar although a good deal changed, and he went on to explain. He had been busking on the street around the Barras to prop up a heroin addiction when a camera crew took a cut-away shot of him playing and moved on, an incident which he promptly forgot. Eventually, the heroin led him into Barlinnie jail for petty theft – and, on Easter Sunday morning, for want of something better to do, he attended the service which included a showing of *The Glasgow Gospel* on a giant screen. There he was churning out *Knocking on Heaven's Door*! In addition to this, the sermon included Pilate's words: 'it is within my power to release a prisoner unto you …' (John 18:39). On returning to his cell, he was given the news that he was being released – and this combination of astounding events led to some serious thought about himself, his situation, his responsibilities and above all, his deliverance. Today, free from both jail and heroin, he pursues Christian work in and out of prison – a walking testament to answered prayer. Unknown to the three men saying a vague 'Amen' in the Barrowland office, God's answer was being poured down on the life of a street busker outside, some thirty yards away.

18

Entrepreneur

In 1995, I had an entrepreneurial urge. I love that word. It sounds dramatic. John Smith, the Glasgow chairman of Save the Children, liked the suggestion that we should hold a Burns Supper in aid of the charity. We formed a small committee. The Hilton Hotel was booked for 26 January 1996, and the planning began. My good friend David Hardman agreed to be chairman at the Supper after I suggested that his car-hire firm should subsidise the event to the tune of £5,000. He obliged. I invited Jimmie McGregor to present the Immortal Memory. Anne Linstrum, Alastair McDonald and Peter Morrison were the singers. Jimmy Black proposed the Toast to the Lassies, and the Reverend Lorna Hood replied to it. My own party pieces completed the programme. It was a gey noisy supper. I wouldn't say that our guests were out of control. Let's state that they were decidedly fleein! Never mind – we raised £12,000 for Save the Children.

The following year, I received an invitation from Lord Provost Pat Lally to recite at his first charity Burns Supper at the Thistle Hotel on 24 January. It was a prestigious event. Ruth Wishart and Brian Meek were fine speakers, and Linda Ormiston sang sweetly. The address to The Haggis was my first slot, followed by 'Holy Willie's Prayer'. Audiences vary, and their behaviour can never be predicted, especially when the drams are being knocked back. However, I must say that the atmosphere at Provost Lally's Burns Supper was incredibly satisfying for me. There were 800 guests in the banqueting room. In order that the folk in the far corners could see the action, there were two enormous video screens in operation. I felt more like Rod Stewart than Jamie Stuart.

I've heard people say that Robert Burns was not a man of God. How wrong can they be? Our national Bard certainly knew his Bible and studied it well. He wrote to his father in 1781, saying that he was inspired by chapter 7 of Revelation: 'and God shall wipe away the tears from their eyes'. In a letter to Peter Hill in 1790, he confesses: 'God knows I am no saint: I have a whole host of follies and sins to answer for; but if I could, and I believe I do it as far as I can, I would wipe away all tears from all eyes.' Robert Burns could certainly deliver a fine sermon; he would have made a guid meenister. In his poem *Tam o' Shanter*, he warns of the temptation of the demon drink and wenches wearing cutty sarks.

Without doubt, *Tam o' Shanter* is one of Burns' masterpieces – one of the greatest narrative poems ever produced. It has everything: light and shade, beautiful images, drama, humour and – above all – fast, tremendous excitement. When I'm let loose with *Tam o' Shanter* and giving it laldy, I'm in seventh heaven! Did it get a standing ovation that night? But, of course!

It's nice to get thanks when you do your wee bit for charity, but I must say I was absolutely chuffed when Save the Children invited me to be a guest of HRH the Princess Royal at a reception on board the Royal Yacht *Britannia* before the yacht's decommissioning. The Clyde-built vessel was berthed back home in Glasgow. This, of course, was not the first time that one of the Stuart boys had been on board. Decades later, I couldn't wait to follow in my big brother's footsteps. The occasion was attended by people who had given their time and talents in aid of Save the Children. After the drinks and canapés and the formal speeches, Tony Roper, of *Rab C. Nesbitt* fame, was in great form as he did his 'turn'. Everyone was presented to the Princess – and 'yours truly' was in the queue. What should I say? I took a chance and asked the Princess if she could remember a certain incident at the 75th

Anniversary luncheon of Save the Children in the Hilton Hotel in 1994. I was privileged enough to be seated at the top table with her that day and was asked to say grace and to announce the sale of raffle tickets. My minister of the time bought a ticket for his wife, Linda. It was a winner, and great cheers rang out when Linda went up to be congratulated by Princess Anne and to be given her prize – a handsome presentation Caithness glass decanter of malt whisky! HRH well remembered the occasion; and I remember that she asked if the minister's wife had told the congregation. The late Tom Fleming (the television and radio broadcaster) chipped in nicely: 'Well, for sure, ma'am, it was a spiritual occasion.'

19

Two More Books

In 1993, I was invited by Saint Andrew Press to write some Old Testament stories in my own particular style. I concentrated to a fair extent on the present-day urban Scots dialect of Glasgow. However, it's a blessing that our Scots speech is fluid and certainly not lacking in variety. I therefore tried to give expression to the various dialects spoken in Scotland. Once again I got my head down, and this time steeped myself in the wonderful stories of the Old Testament. I studied every translation I could find, and referred to many commentaries. It was also helpful to read condensed versions and children's bibles. My friend Dr John Drane, then of Stirling University, whose writings about the Bible are internationally acclaimed, agreed to meet me and talk. 'I've no doubt you'll be choosing the entertaining stories like "In the Beginning", "Joseph", "David and Goliath" and "Jonah",' he smiled. 'Correct, John: yes, I had decided on them.' 'Well, I'll not fault you there, Jamie, but I'd strongly suggest that you include the story of Job. That'll give you something to think about.' I took John Drane's advice and studied the Book of Job. It is very deep! In his book *A Beginner's Guide to the Old Testament*, Professor Robert Davidson comments on the Book of Job:

It has been called one of the greatest marvels and mysteries in the literature of the world. If we have any sensitivity to language, we can do no other than marvel at the Book of Job. Chapters 38–42 contain two speeches from God to Job, speeches worthy of the God who is the source of all poetry. They have seldom, if ever, been surpassed in literature.

I felt that I could manage a beginning and an ending to my presentation, but I baulked at the speeches from God to Job. They were too difficult for me to handle. So, what did I do? I said a prayer. The answer came right away. I remembered that my good friend Dr Robert Stephen, the Buchan poet, had presented the story of Job in verse. I contacted him, and he granted me permission to use the relevant verses to complete my presentation. After finishing my chapter on Job, I decided to include the following stories: In the Beginning; Joseph; Gideon; Ruth; David and Goliath; Elisha; Esther; Daniel; and Jonah. *Auld Testament Tales* was published in October 1993 and went into the top ten bestsellers' list.

My new minister, the Reverend John Hegarty, wrote the book's cover review:

The fascination of a kaleidoscope attracts the attention of adult and child alike: individual pieces fall together to form an attractive pattern. The first part of the Bible, the Old Testament, is just such a kaleidoscope of word pictures – tales told and retold down through the centuries. The language can change, order can be rearranged, but the stories remain the same. From the startling colours of Joseph's coat to the poignancy of the story of Ruth, Jamie Stuart has used the language of today to make the colour of each tale sparkle afresh. His kaleidoscope produces a picture that is fascinating and compelling.

Professor Robert Davidson wrote the Foreword to *Auld Testament Tales*, and ended with:

I have just one quibble. Some of my favourite stories have not been given the treatment. What about Abraham ... Jacob

... Moses ... Samuel ... Saul ... Elijah ... Solomon ... Nehe-miah ...? There is a rich seam here still waiting to be mined. I hope the success of this first selection of Auld Testament stories will encourage and challenge Jamie to have another go. 'Lang may his lum reek' as he continues to entertain and teach.

It had not occurred to me that my work would be considered entertaining; but that's fine. The Good Book says: 'A merry heart doeth good like a medicine' (Proverbs 17:22).

When, in 1997, Lesley Taylor of Saint Andrew Press asked me for more copy, I took the hint from the Professor and pro-duced the stories he had requested, plus Isaac and Samson. Saint Andrew Press then decided to combine the two lots of Old Testament Stories, plus the full text of *The Glasgow Gospel*. We entitled the collection *A Glasgow Bible*. Once again, the book went into the bestsellers' list. It has since had many reprints, such has been the global interest.

Do I believe that prayers are answered? Yes! I do!

On the morning of the launch of *A Glasgow Bible*, I was interviewed live on the BBC television news. No matter how much one tries to prepare, live TV is a scary experience. Sitting alone in a tiny studio in Queen Margaret Drive in Glasgow, I was interviewed by Liz McKean from London. She introduced me to the listeners: 'Now, today sees the launch of a new publi-cation of the Bible. It's been written by Jamie Stuart, who is an elder in the Church of Scotland.'

I was requested to read from my book, and chose the passage about David and Goliath, as follows: 'Goliath, the big man, dauners up tae Davie, an looks him up an doon. Then he raps oan his shield wi the end o his spear. "Are *you* the best they've got?" he sneers. "Weel, come oan then, ya scrawny plook. An by my ain god, Dagon, ah'll cut ye up for the sparras!"' Liz said she rather liked that, and smiled. 'Just one thing, Jamie. What is a "scrawny plook"?' I explained that it meant a 'frail wee pimple'.

I had the opportunity to say that Prince Charles had been speaking the week before and had commented on the majesty of the Authorised Version of the Bible – and I agreed with him. 'Yes indeed,' I said, 'the King James translation of the Bible has great majesty, dignity and lyrical beauty, but it's the language of 400 years ago, and it does not always communicate clearly. Regional dialects have now become more acceptable than they were some years ago. Perhaps Sean Connery had something to do with it. In *A Glasgow Bible*, the vernacular is pungent, powerful and totally accessible.'

The launch of *A Glasgow Bible* took place in Wesley Owen's bookshop in Buchanan Street, Glasgow on Thursday 8 May 1997, when a dozen of my friends gave dramatised readings of the various chapters.

The highlight of the morning came in one of the Joseph stories. The manager of the shop, Mary McLeod, played the scheming wife of Potiphar attempting to seduce the hapless Joseph. We had no rehearsals. One of my best pals was cast as Joseph, but little did he suspect how *passionately* Mary would act!

20

Daisy's Big Day

One of my previous occupations was acting as a voluntary tour guide at the Glasgow Royal Concert Hall. It was my pleasant job to escort parties of visitors around the entire Concert Hall complex. On my first tour, I led about fifty people, and on arrival at the upstairs foyer I identified photographs on the wall of various conductors and soloists.

As an elder in my local church, I visit the housebound members of our congregation; and I once invited an old friend of mine to take the tour. Mrs Daisy Currie, a widow living on her own, was, during her time as a member of High Carntyne Parish Church, the leading soprano in our church choir for many years. At 93 years of age, she had become rather slow and was finding it difficult to walk very far. Her hearing and speech were reasonable, but her sight had all but left her. She was delighted to be invited to join the tour, but wondered if the walking would be too much. I informed her that she could use one of the wheelchairs at the Concert Hall. She wasn't too keen on this suggestion until I made it clear that she could get up from time to time to show people that she was not confined to a wheelchair.

'Well, that seems just fine, James. Can Jean come too?' she asked.

I told her that I would arrange the date with her pal Jean.

The day arrived, and I picked up my two friends in a taxi, and we arrived at the Concert Hall. About twenty people were waiting to take the one-hour guided tour.

'Good afternoon, ladies and gentlemen, my name is Jamie

Stuart and I am your tour guide for today.' At this point, I enquired of my party if they had been to the Hall before, and also asked where they came from. On this particular day, we had a few folk from Glasgow and the rest from England, Ireland, Italy and the USA. I proceeded to lead the group from the south entrance, through the 600-capacity exhibition hall, which doubles as the main foyer, then to the inner foyers and up the grand staircase to the Strathclyde Suite. This hall can also take 600 patrons. The suite is used for concerts, films, conferences, weddings and the like.

We then moved into the lovely restaurant and cocktail bar, and from the circle entrance into the magnificent 2,500-capacity auditorium. The party was invited to take a seat, and all the features of the hall were explained.

'Well now, ladies and gentlemen. Would you like to view Shirley Bassey's five-star dressing room?' I asked.

Everyone always wants to see the dressing rooms, especially the stars' double dressing room – one room for the visitors and an inner sanctum for dressing, complete with huge mirrors and grand piano. On leaving the dressing rooms, we proceeded past the stage-manager's control point and finally onto the stage.

'Well, ladies and gentlemen, here we are on the stage of the Glasgow Royal Concert Hall,' I announce. 'Since we opened our doors in August 1990 we've heard many fine orchestras. As well as our own Royal Scottish National Orchestra and the City of Glasgow Philharmonic Orchestra, we have hosted famous orchestras and singers from all over the world. Recently, I'm proud to say we have been enthralled by the glorious singing of Jessye Norman and Montserrat Caballé.'

My party seem to be impressed by my spiel, and I catch the eye of Mrs Currie.

'I might say, ladies and gentlemen, that Mrs Currie here was the leading soprano in High Carntyne Church for many years.'

At this point, Daisy has risen from the wheelchair and is standing on the stage with the rest of the party. She is a small lady, smartly dressed, with a neat hairstyle and blue eyes, and is a very alert 93 years 'young', although rather shaky and almost blind.

'Could I sing now, James?' she whispers to me, and smiles.

I didn't hesitate. 'Ladies and gentlemen,' I intimated, 'Daisy Currie is going to favour us with a song!'

Daisy winked at me and moved slowly forward so that she was slightly side-on to the group and to the 2,500 empty seats.

This is my lovely day
This is the day I shall
Remember the day I'm dying ...

She gave out the whole song clearly and sweetly. The lady from Chicago wiped away her tears. Daisy's audience of twenty gave her a hearty round of applause.

Returning home in the taxi, she turned to me and to Jean: 'Well, Jamie – I think this must be one of the happiest days of my life. I can now say that I've sung in the Glasgow Royal Concert Hall.'

'You certainly can,' I answered. 'And you got a big round of applause.'

Shortly after her visit to the Concert Hall, Daisy died peacefully at a local nursing home. She was a lady to be admired.

On the Sunday after her 'performance' at the Concert Hall, our minister had greeted her: 'Well, good morning Mrs Currie, and congratulations. I believe your debut at the Concert Hall was a great success.'

As she took her seat in the kirk that morning, I could almost hear her singing to herself:

This is my lovely day
This is the day I shall
Remember the day I'm dying ...

21

An Osculant Occasion

Early in 2013, I was invited by my friend the Reverend Jim Martin (no relation to my former minister, the Reverend James Martin) of Kilsyth Church to give readings in his church hall.

It was an informal evening of Christian fellowship with hymn-singing, songs and readings. We had an attendance of about 100 folk of all ages. The atmosphere was very friendly and relaxed, with lively music from guitars and drums.

I gave readings from my *Auld Testament Tales* book and then some stories from *The Glasgow Gospel*. My final part of the evening was a presentation, from memory, of the Prodigal Son.

The late Professor William Barclay reckoned that it was the greatest short story ever written, but felt that it should have been called 'The Loving Father'. He goes on to explain:

It was by no means unusual for a father to distribute his estate before he died if he wished to retire from the actual management of affairs, but there is a certain heartless callousness in the request of the younger son. He said, in effect, 'Give me now the part of the estate I will get anyway when you are dead, and let me out of this'.

The father did not argue. He knew that if the son was ever to learn, he must learn the hard way, and he granted his request. Without delay, the son realised his share of the property and left home.

He soon ran through the money and finished up feeding pigs. He then decided to come home and plead to be taken back, but not as a son, but in the lowest rank of slaves.

The father must have been waiting and watching for his son to come home, for he saw him a long way off. When he came, he forgave him with no recriminations.

Once, Abraham Lincoln was asked how he was going to treat the rebellious Southerners when they had finally been defeated and returned to the Union of the United States. The questioner had expected that Lincoln would take dire vengeance, but he answered: 'I will treat them as if they had never been away'.

That is not the end of the story.

There enters the elder brother, who was actually sorry that his brother had come home. He stands for the self-righteous Pharisees who would rather see a sinner destroyed than saved.

The father's love included both brothers. His forgiving love symbolises the divine Mercy of God.

So, here I am in Kilsyth Church hall giving my presentation of the Prodigal Son. I can never forecast the reaction of the audience to this powerful and emotive story.

As I narrate the parable in the ordinary language of the Scottish people, it really seems to come alive – in a different way from tellings in the Authorised Version of the Bible or other modern translations.

As a former professional actor, I find it impossible to just tell the story – I have to dramatise the piece. I've presented this story many times, and at the conclusion there are always tears in my eyes. I wait for about ten seconds and then say 'Amen'. Sometimes there is dead silence, and on other occasions much applause. It certainly is a moving story. On this evening, there is applause.

Jim Martin then comes forward and pats me on the back. 'Well done, wee man', he says.

Several others in the hall come forward and say how much they enjoyed the stories.

Then it happens!!

A very attractive middle-aged lady comes forward and thanks me. 'Oh my goodness, Mr Stuart, that was very emotional. What can I say?' Then she gives me a lasting kiss – on the lips! And thanks me again. (Later, I establish from Jim Martin that the lady is one of his members and a person of good manners and sound mind.)

Several more people shake my hand and congratulate me – and then, just as I am trying to regain a sense of calm, the aforementioned lady comes forward, again, thanks me for coming, and kisses me!

Now, at this point I want to make something very clear: the contacts made upon me were not just wee cheepers. They were well-directed, sincere SMACKERS. Was I embarrassed? Did I resist?

All I can confess is that, as an elderly widower of over thirty years, I am not usually the recipient of such amorous advances. Nevertheless, I might just ask the Reverend Jim Martin to invite me back to Kilsyth.

22

A Mountain Too Far

Ben Lomond wis nae bother. I had climbed it twice as a laddie.
I had also got to within 100 yards of the summit of Ben Nevis
when the mist came down. During my time in the RAF, while
stationed at Cairo West, I had scaled Khufu, the highest
pyramid of the pharaohs. So, Kilimanjaro should be a doddle!

Okay, what's the story? My 21-year-old friend, David Blair,
greeted me. 'Jamie, I'm very excited!' he exclaimed. 'Carol and
I have received funding, and in three months' time we are off to
climb Kilimanjaro to raise money for Christian Aid.' David and
Carol were experienced young hillwalkers and were well prepared for such a challenge. I had a good chat with my friends
and wished them well. Turning over in my bed that night, I
said to myself: 'Yes, why not join them?' Kilimanjaro! What
an adventure! Kilimanjaro!! Even the name sounds dramatic. I
could see my photie in the *Sunday Post* with the banner head-
line: 'Diminutive Glasgow Geriatric Conquers Kilimanjaro!' I
was only 65 at the time and as fit as a fiddle.

Kilimanjaro is an extinct volcano in Tanzania. At 19,340
feet, it is the highest mountain in Africa. Its lower slopes are
intensely cultivated, coffee and bananas being the chief crops.
I knew that it was not reckoned to be an extremely dangerous
mountain to climb and that there was a well-worn trail to the
peak. I would not need an ice-pick. So – the decision was made!
I would now require funding for the flight, the hotel and the
necessary equipment. Who did I know who would support me?
Yes indeed – the very man! – Mr Stepek.

My old boss Jan Stepek was a successful entrepreneur. He had a string of television shops and travel centres, and business was going well. For 12 years I had been his most successful manager in terms of sales figures; and he held me in high regard. At that time, Mr Stepek was semi-retired and spent many months playing golf in Florida. His son Richard was in charge of the 'shop'. I often reminded him that at the Christmas parties – as Santa Claus – I had given him his presents. Surely Richard would not let me down.

In due course we met, and he welcomed my desire to raise money for my favourite charity, Save the Children. 'Jamie, I wish you well,' he smiled. 'I hope you make it. Please send me an estimate for the flights, hotel and the gear. I will send you a cheque for the amount.'

David and Carol and I met several times to pore over maps and trails and to plan for our great adventure. The date of departure was getting near. I honestly felt that I was doing the right thing, but I decided to keep it quiet from my family until nearer the flight time. A few weeks before our departure, Carol phoned me on a Sunday morning to arrange a meeting with David and to book the flights. My daughter Fiona was home at the time. It was a Sunday at 10:30am, and we were about to leave for the church service. I took the call downstairs, and spoke quietly. Fiona was upstairs.

We left our house, bound for the kirk, and Fiona spoke first. 'You're usually so loud on the phone, Dad. Was that a big secret you were discussing?' I took a huge breath, filling both lungs and my diaphragm. 'Well, yes, it was a bit of a secret. I was about to tell you very soon.' I then endeavoured to explain what I was about to do along with my friends, and tried to make it sound as if we were going for a jog in the local park. Our church is only five minutes' walk from our house. There was silence for a while. I was looking straight ahead, and my diaphragm was working overtime. I knew that Fiona was looking at me.

'Da-ad', she said in a kind of sympathetic tone of voice.

'Yes, dear?' I said.

'Da-ad, you are *not* going to be climbing Kilimanjaro.'

'Oh,' I said. 'Really?'

'Yes, Dad, really,' said my daughter. We both smiled. End of story.

P.S. It seemed a good idea at the time.

23

Peace of Mind

I was reading an article in a magazine, and it gave three hints on how to be happy and have peace of mind. First of all, it said, one must go into a quiet room and think on happy experiences while stroking one's cat! – and breathe deeply.

Secondly, it advised one to laugh as much as possible, as laughing is good for the body and soul. Thirdly, it said, it's good to sing when the occasion arises.

I decide that the next time I present 'An evening with Jamie Stuart', I'll try out these suggestions.

'Right then, folks', I say, 'we all want peace of mind. It's dead easy. Breathe deeply, stroke your cat – have a laugh and sing a song.'

I get my audience to stand up, lift their arms slowly up and down, and breathe deeply – three times. Then I go for the laughter. I put on a serious face and say: 'Now, chums. I want everybody to smile!' It works! It's amazing! My audience start looking at each other, smiling, and then start laughing.

I tell them their laughter does not satisfy me. So, I then put on a schoolboy cap and say: 'This morning, I got a letter from my mother. This is what she says:

Dear Son, There have been a few changes since you were home last. Granny has had all her teeth out and a new gas stove put in.

Your wee cousin Hector is not well again. It's his head. He's had it on and off ever since he was born.

Actually, I've not been very well, son. To tell you the truth, I've been in bed for a week with the doctor.

Also, I've been getting a wee bit deaf. Got some medicine for it – took a big dose last night and this morning I heard from your uncle in Australia!

(Sorry about this drivel, folks – but at least it's wholesome drivel. Where was I?)

Last night, we went to a party, son. It was great. Everybody had to pretend to be a country. Wee Hector put a chamber-pot on his head and said he was China, but your father won easy. He took his trousers down and said he was Chile. Bye for now.

Your Loving Mother.

P.S. I meant to put a ten-pound note in with this, but I've already sealed down the envelope.

'Now we come to the singing, folks. Everybody please stand up.' They all stand up. 'Right – all together now. Sing "Jesus Loves Me".' After the first few lines, I say: 'STOP! STOP! STOP! – SIT DOWN, that was terrible! If you're going to sing "Jesus Loves Me", you must let the whole of Glasgow (or Bellshill, or Govan) know that Jesus loves you. Now stand up.' They all get up again and sing with gusto.

'Well done! Sit down,' I say. 'Thanks for coming. Safe home! Love your neighbour! Goodnight.'

24

A Scot Abroad

I often receive letters from overseas readers of *The Glasgow Gospel* and *A Scots Gospel*. There is a huge interest in North America in all things Scottish.

A few years ago, I received the following letter from Pennsylvania:

Dear Mr Stuart, I am sending this letter c/o your minister since I do not have your home address. I have just received a gift copy of your book *The Glasgow Gospel* and am writing to congratulate you on a significant work. You have captured the authentic spirit of the Gospel and expressed it in the music of Glasgow which was the music of my own soul – so long ago. I was born in Glasgow eighty-one years ago and am now retired in the United States, where I served as a preacher for over twenty-six years.

Under separate cover I am mailing to you my autobiography, *I've Seen the Day*.

Concerning the Scots language, you and I know that translations and renderings are legion: Aberdeenshire (my mither's tongue) is not only different from the Borders but also has a different vocabulary; different from the Highlands, where they are translating from the Gaelic idiom as they speak.

I have two Scots translations of the scriptures – the Reverend William W. Smith's *The New Testament in Braid Scots* and the more modern book, William Lorimer's *The New Testament in Scots*.

The problem which both of these writers had to face (and

did not succeed very well) was to choose the idiom, vocabulary and mode of expression of a dialect that would be acceptable to all Scots. There was also what I call the failure of the more academic scholars to publish the hybrid called the 'Lallans'. The fact is that each community, Borders, Ayrshire, Lothians, Aberdeenshire and the West Highlands have their own distinct dialect – brought about by the fact that for centuries there was hardly any intercommunication between these parts of Scotland.

What you have done – bless you – is to choose one area – Glasgow – and to paraphrase the text in the language of the Glaswegian, and that is splendid!

The Galilean accent (which was the Aramaic dialect of our Lord) was looked upon as rather rural by the educated Scribes and Pharisees of Jerusalem. With all due reverence, it is conceivable that our Lord spoke a dialect which could be likened to the Glasgow Speak?

Wherefore my congratulations!

Warmly and with every blessing.

George M. Docherty

George's book *I've Seen the Day* is a brilliant story. I was fascinated to learn that he was the person responsible for having the phrase 'under God' inserted into the American Pledge of Allegiance – this Church of Scotland minister born in a room and kitchen in Hathaway Street, Maryhill, Glasgow.

In his book, he relates that, while he was struggling for a topic for a sermon to be preached in his charge, the prestigious Church of the Presidents in Washington DC, his son came home from school, and they began to discuss the events of the day. The Pledge of Allegiance came up during the course of the conversation, and it suddenly occurred to George Docherty that there was no reference to God in it.

'I had found my sermon', he says; and he went on to present it to a congregation that just happened to include the then President of the USA, Dwight D. Eisenhower.

(In his time, George Docherty has also preached on moral courage to Richard Nixon during the Watergate crisis, and marched with Martin Luther King in Selma, Alabama.)

His sermon was reported in the national press and provoked such a flood of support that the words 'under God' were officially inserted in the Pledge of Allegiance on 14 June 1954.

George Docherty was born in Glasgow in 1911 and was ordained in the Church of Scotland. He dedicated his book to the congregations of Ruchill, Glasgow; King's Park, Glasgow; the Barony of Glasgow; and the North Kirk, Aberdeen. He then spent the major part of his career as pastor of the New York Avenue Presbyterian Church in Washington, DC.

He accepted the call to serve that church in 1950, succeeding Peter Marshall, and remained there until his retirement in 1975.

George Docherty's personal life is also revealed in his book: the formative years in Scotland, showing the influences of family and friends, professors and churchmen; the births of three children, and the sudden death of his wife Jerry in 1970; his subsequent marriage to Sue; and the births of two more daughters in the 'autumn of his days'. George died peacefully at home in 2008. He was 97 years old.

25

Wise Words

At the beginning of 2006, I had itchy writing fingers, and I wondered what I could do to encourage people to appreciate the Scots language. We all know that the authorised King James Version of the Bible and the works of Shakespeare are regarded as the greatest literary works in the English language – but the language of over 400 years ago is not always easily understood by young people today.

I reckoned that it might be an interesting exercise to compare some Proverbs from the Good Book and place them side by side with my own rendering in the twenty-first-century language of many ordinary Scots folk.

This would also give me the chance to study the book of Proverbs. It's all there – advice on money, power, marriage, friendship, health, sleep, jealousy, war, peace and eternity. It's full to the brim of pithy wisdom.

However, it is not the easiest of books in the Bible to understand. It is long; it comes from different sources; it often repeats what it has already said. Yet it contains much of value, with shrewd comments on life, and with sound and stimulating advice. It has come down to us in a variety of different translations. Some of the language is 'gey strange' – very different from what we use in our language today.

Here are some pairings from my publication *Proverbs in the Patter* (Saint Andrew Press).

Take fast hold of instruction; let her not go: keep her;	*Tak a close grip o guid coonsel; dinnae let her awa;*

for she is thy life.

(4:13)

haud her; for she's the very
life o' ye.

A wise son maketh a glad
father: but a foolish son is
the heaviness of his mother.

(10:1)

A son wha keeps the heid
will please his faither, but
a rebel boy gies his maw a
hard time.

As the whirlwind passeth,
so is the wicked no more:
but the righteous is an
everlasting foundation.

(10:25)

The blast o the storm blaws
the wicked clean oot o sight.
Guid folk are aye safe wi the
Lord for their anchor.

As vinegar to the teeth, and
as smoke to the eyes, so is
the sluggard to them that
send him.

(10:26)

Like vinegar seepin aboot the
mooth, an like smoke reekin
tae the een, so is the lazy lout
a pain in the behouchie tae
the honest folk wha hiv tae
thole him.

When pride cometh, then
cometh shame: but with the
lowly is wisdom.

(11:2)

Where there's pride, there's
a faw no far awa. Modest folk
tend tae keep the heid.

Riches profit not in the day
of wrath: but righteousness
delivereth from death.

(11:4)

Aw the gear in the world will
be nae use on judgement day.
The Maister will check yer
morals!

There is that maketh himself
rich, yet hath nothing: there
is that maketh himself poor,
yet hath great riches.

(13:7)

A person can become rich, but
yet hiv nothin; some poor
bodies hiv great wealth.

The light of the righteous rejoiceth: but the lamp of the wicked shall be put out. (13:9)	*The light in the guid folk shines brightly; the leeries o the wicked shall be snuffed oot.*
The mouth of strange women is a deep pit: he that is abhorred of the Lord shall fall therein. (22:14)	*The mooth o an ill-daein wumman is like a deep sheuch. Wha disnae gie respect tae the Lord'll faw intae it!*
Make no friendship with an angry man; and with a furious man thou shalt not go: lest thou learn his ways, and get a snare to thy soul. (22:24–5)	*Dinnae mak friens wi a short-tempered bodie, an keep oot o the road o the crabbit; or else ye might copy them an get a girn aboot yer face.*
These six things doth the Lord hate: yea, seven are an abomination unto him: A proud look, a lying tongue, and hands that shed innocent blood, An heart that deviseth wicked imaginations, feet that be swift in running to mischief, A false witness that speaketh lies, and he that soweth discord among brethren. (6:16–19)	*Here's sax things that the Lord'll hae nane o – deed-aye, there's seeven that He detests awthegither: boastfu een, a leein tongue, hauns that herm the feckless, a hert that's aye ettlin evil, feet runnin aff tae gie trouble, a crooked witness tellin lees, an the bodie wha sows bickerin amang brithers.*

26

The Glasgow Gospel DVD

I was pleased that my good friend Glen Collie agreed to undertake a film production of my work. Here are his comments:

> Autumn 2009 saw the release of an entirely new DVD version of *The Glasgow Gospel*. The film was based on *A Glasgow Bible*, and the Scots tongue was interpreted through unique performances from a marvellous cast who contributed unstintingly of their time and talents. Collie Productions produced the DVD over the preceding eighteen months. It was a mammoth task to complete thirty-four individual segments, retelling the Christian story in locations in and around Glasgow.
>
> The feature-length programme contained performances by a diverse and numerous cast of weel-kent faces, a grand selection of ministers and a variety of talented 'real people'.

Featured among the cast of forty-four actors were John Cairney, Mary Marquis, Eileen McCallum, Alastair McDonald, Peter Morrison, Tony Roper, the Reverend Alec Shuttleworth, Donald Smith and myself. Glen goes on:

> Alastair McDonald created and interpreted the musical score as well as delivering 'Fishers o Men'.
>
> As part of their celebration of 200 years of 'Taking the Word to the World', the Scottish Bible Society commissioned a short promotional DVD featuring six of the segments from the full *Glasgow Gospel* DVD. 75,000 copies were distributed in the *Herald* newspaper.

When asked what was the 'best' part of the filming, Jane Collie, the producer, highlighted the fact that, during the entire production, which was filmed in dozens of locations, everyone embraced the spirit of the project and allowed extraordinary access to film in their locations.

27

Last Man Standing

In June 2011, I noticed a photograph of myself (at the age of 27 years) in the *Herald* newspaper, and sent off a letter to the editor. The newspaper receives so many letters that the staff don't have the time to acknowledge each one.

However, the day after I sent the account of my theatre memory, my letter resulted in a headline, and my story.

My part in an epic production that revitalised Scottish theatre

Friday 24 June 2011

I was interested to see myself in your photograph of *Ane Satyre of The Thrie Estaits* production staged in Edinburgh in 1948 ('Estaits of the nation', *The Herald*, June 21).

At 90 years of age, I'm probably the last living member of that epic production.

The Thrie Estaits by Sir David Lindsay was first performed at Linlithgow in January 1540, before the King and Queen. The second production was at Cupar, Fife in 1552. Another presentation was given at Calton Hill, Edinburgh in 1554. At the time the play was written, Lindsay was about 54. He had studied at St Andrews and afterwards entered the Royal household, as Lord Lyon, King at Arms, and an envoy. The play so enraged the Scottish clergy of the time that they ordered the manuscript to be burned by the public executioner in 1558, three years after the author's death.

In the autumn of 1948, the entire company of the Glasgow Citizens' Theatre was involved in a memorable enterprise. Playwright James Bridie, producer Tyrone Guthrie and Festival director Rudolph Bing planned the project. It was a joint theatrical presentation between the Citizens' Theatre, Unity, Dundee and Perth Repertory Companies. The playwright Robert Kemp was commissioned to adapt the text, and Tyrone Guthrie (later to be knighted) directed the play.

The first objective was to find a hall large enough to encompass the complex staging requirements. Eventually it was suggested that the Church of Scotland Assembly Hall at the top of the Mound might be worth examination. Tyrone Guthrie knew he was home as soon as the gaunt silhouette of the twin-towered hall loomed into view in the shadow of the historic castle, high above and far removed from the bottom of Princes Street.

In all, there were thirty-two speaking parts. Forty-eight extras played members of the Estates, townsfolk and soldiers. In addition, there were singers and musicians, making it a vast undertaking. I was cast in one of the principal roles, Sandy Solace, the inebriated courtier. The character was described as rumbustious and loud-mouthed – which suited me fine.

On Tuesday 24 August 1948, under Guthrie's inspired direction, the long-dormant play sprang to renewed life. No-one could have predicted its phenomenal success.

One newspaper declared: 'The whole cast is obviously in love with what it is doing, and there is such uniform excellence of playing that it seems almost ungrateful to mention individual actors. But Duncan Macrae's wonderful clowning in the dual role of Flatterie and the Pardoner was a masterpiece of a flavour as Scottish as whisky. But the real triumph was in the wonderful direction. It is nothing less than a landmark in the history of the European Theatre.'

The production became the smash-hit of the Festival. There was a resurgence of pride in the Scottish theatre. James Bridie was justifiably proud of his Glasgow Citizens' people, who had not only played the leading roles but had also supplied both management and production teams. Characteristically impish, he indulged in a little exaggeration in a lecture to the Royal Philosophical Society of Glasgow, claiming that the play was now the talk of the civilised world.

Jamie Stuart

The recollection of my part in the play was prompted by an article in the *Herald* by a journalist, Neil Cooper. He reported that the writer, Paul Henderson Scott, had been campaigning for years to have *The Satire* revived once more for a current generation.

Mr Scott's clarion call for action did not go unheeded. In June 2013, a major production of *The Satire* was performed at Linlithgow Palace, where the original version had taken place in 1540. The production was part of a major research project funded by the Arts and Humanities Research Council which explored the historical and contemporary significance of Lindsay's play and the political and material culture which produced it. The event was a collaboration between a team of university scholars, together with actors drawn from the Scottish theatre community.

The play was staged in the open air in the grounds of the palace, and was a huge success. Not content with that, in the following week the company staged a smaller version of the play in the Great Hall of Stirling Castle. There was an eerie kind of atmosphere that night in Stirling; the castle ghosts must have been grinning when hearing the debates in the guid Scots tongue.

Why am I so lucky? I was requested to give a rendering from my character in the play – Sandy Solace – and, remembering the lines without difficulty, gave vent to Sandy.

Did I hear a murmur from the rafters? Maybe it was Auld Nick mouthing: 'Gaun yersel, wee man!'

28

Seven Days of Heaven

It was early August 2010. 'Hello Jamie, how are you? This is Ann speaking. I have news for you.'

'Good to hear your voice, Ann. Is it exciting news?' It certainly was interesting news: Ann Crawford, the publishing manager of Saint Andrew Press (Church of Scotland), had received a call from a band leader based in Nashville, Tennessee. He worked with Trinity Broadcasting International (TBI), which claims to be the biggest Christian television broadcaster in the USA with a potential audience of over 50 million viewers. The caller's name was Ric Blair. Ric had been commissioned by TBI to produce a film entitled *A Celtic Christmas*. It would be presented in front of a live audience of 1,200 in August, broadcast at Christmas, and then released as a commercial DVD.

The plan was to present a two-hour musical feature which would be appropriate for the Christmas season and be firmly based in the Celtic tradition.

Two years previously, Ric had been touring Scotland with his band – and, while appearing in Dundee, his drummer, John Kincaid, was browsing in a bookshop and had spotted *A Glasgow Bible*. Opening it, he read some pages and turned to Ric. 'Look at this, boss,' he exclaimed. 'This would fit in nicely for the Celtic Christmas that you keep talking about.' Ric scanned the pages. 'You're so right, John. The King James Bible would be too formal to blend with our music, and the Irish Gaelic might be too challenging for our audience. This rendering is exciting and totally accessible.'

Hence the phone call to Ann Crawford. Ric explained the plan for the film and requested permission to use *A Glasgow Bible*. Ann was happy to accept the call, and readily agreed to give permission for the use of our publication. She then mentioned that Jamie Stuart was a professional actor and had memorised the Christmas story from the book. 'Well, well, indeed,' said Ric. 'Do you think he would be willing to talk to me?' This conversation happened on a Saturday. For the next six days, I glanced at my phone. And then – on the Saturday morning, I got a call. 'Hello! Am I speaking to Mr Jamie Stooart? You probably know what I'm going to ask you.' I told him that I guessed the reason for his call. He invited me to take part in the concert, and we talked about how I would fit in.

I would soon be flying out to the USA. Sure enough, the necessary flight documents were sent to me in the post, and I was all set to go. My son-in-law Martin drove me to Glasgow Airport, and in due course I arrived in the state of rock 'n' roll. It could have been Memphis, but Nashville would do. At the airport reception, I was met by a very tall man ready with his taxi. 'Hello there man, am I speaking to Jamie from England?' I corrected him, and we got on like a house on fire on the two-mile journey to the outskirts of Nashville. I arrived at a very classy hotel, got my key from reception and settled into my room with a huge sense of relief. It had been a tiring journey.

Within minutes, there was a knock at the door – and I admitted the producer of the film, George Telford by name. He was in charge of the casting, the stage set, the crew, the publicity and so on, and had a good working relationship with Ric Blair. We made coffee and had a great chat, and he asked to hear a bit of my rendering for the concert. He seemed delighted – and that gave me a great sense of relief. George was a really bright and cheery individual and put me at my ease right away. 'Now Jamie, here is your ribbon to go round your neck. It's for the restaurant at the auditorium. You will not require to pay for anything – coffee, lunch, dinner etc.; also, for you, there's a free taxi service from here to the theatre, one mile away.'

George stood up to leave – and then pressed a wad of dollars into my hand. I was surprised, because TBI is a charity. There had never been any mention of a fee for my participation. 'My goodness,' I said. I can't remember what else I said. Anyway, I decided not to protest and upset the fellow.

The TBI complex, for me, was one of the wonders of the world. It covered an area of about twenty acres, giving a home to a lovely modern theatre, library, recording studios, offices and a place of worship. Next to the theatre, there was the most attractive small cafe/restaurant. It was a circular structure which could cater for about 100 diners, with 90 per cent of the building having large windows looking out to the gardens. Ah, the gardens! I was reminded of the fabulous Garden Festival in Glasgow in 1988, when people came from all parts of the world to admire the show. The TBI gardens were wonderful. I have never seen better: manicured lawns, waterfalls, miniature statues, wandering streams, attractive grass mounds, small bridges, flowers of every hue beautifully displayed, pools with all manner of goldfish, hanging baskets and tinkling bells. The hydrangea and azalea were gorgeous. And of course the bougainvillea trailing over trellises – dazzling bright and exotic. What a joyful creation! Who says there is no God?

On the Monday morning, I witnessed the band rehearsing. They were brilliant. After lunch, I was sitting outside the cafe talking to George, and I told him how privileged I felt to be part of the event. 'I'm a happy wee man, sir. I really am.' The sun was shining. The temperature was around 80 degrees Fahrenheit, and there was a gentle breeze. I surveyed the colourful gardens. 'George,' I said, 'did I say that I was happy?' He nodded and smiled. I sure was happy. I had been welcomed with open arms by all these lovely American people. Why was God so good to me? I felt so peaceful – the camaraderie of my new friends – the weather – the music – the gardens, all contributed to my mood. It's good to be happy. At that time in Nashville, Tennessee, I was in Paradise.

Ric Blair was multi-talented. He sang, played the piano and

guitar, and was the director. The music group consisted of two main fiddlers, a backing group of seven fiddlers and viola, a keyboard organ, a flute, Irish pipes and two drummers, not forgetting the two tabors. The special guest was Mairéad Ní Mhaonaigh from the Donegal group Altan, considered by many as the best Irish fiddler on the planet. The Riverdance piper was Ivan Goff from Dublin. In the programme, there was also Irish dancing and a children's choir. I had the pleasant honour of compèring the entire show – with, of course, a rendering of the Christmas story, by memory, from my wee book. On Saturday 28 August 2010, *A Celtic Christmas* was performed to an audience of over 1,000 people (with free admission) and received a thunderous standing ovation. The film of the concert was shown worldwide. I'll never forget the experience. Indeed, that was my week of heaven.

29

He Was There

Shortly after returning from America, I went on a cruise holiday with my pal John Burleigh. He lives in Greenock and is the pastor of the Greenock Seaman's Mission. The cruise took us to Norway, Denmark, Sweden, Finland and Russia. However, my abiding memory of that holiday was when we landed in Oslo, Norway, and had four hours to spend before returning to the ship.

In an earlier chapter, I tell how, in May 1945, just after VE Day, my rear-gunner Paddy and I had hitched a lift to Oslo city centre. We made for the Palace and, arriving there, were enthralled to witness a large orchestra and many choirs from throughout the land, singing a welcome home to King Haakon. He had flown in from London, having been exiled there since 1939. The sight of the monarch waving to his people brought tears to the eyes.

Now we must fast-forward sixty-five years, and I'm on that cruise with my pal. Arriving at Oslo, we made our way down the gangway and hailed a taxi. 'John, we're going to the Palace,' I said. 'That's fine by me, Captain,' he smiled. 'You seem to know your way about.' After ten minutes' drive, we arrived at the royal residence, and I recalled being there before and hearing the glorious voices of the choirs welcoming King Haakon home again. Memories, ah memories! We need them; such is life. John and I bought tickets for the tour of the Palace and waited for the French-speaking party to leave.

'Good afternoon, ladies and gentlemen.' The Norwegian lady guide spoke in an impeccable English voice. 'Please follow me.' There were about forty tourists in our group from the USA, Australia and the UK. We were shown all the important places: the public areas, the drawing rooms, the bedrooms, the nursery, the library and the kitchens. Finally, we were shown into the picture gallery, which was the largest hall in the Palace, with fabulous colour murals displayed on the walls. Our friendly guide described many of the pictures. 'And now,' she said, 'this is my favourite.' She pointed to a very large painting in vivid colours. 'This is a depiction of the welcome home to our king in the month of May 1945. Ladies and gentlemen, you can see him on the balcony waving to his people. Note how many people are on the concourse. They were choirs who came from many parts to sing happy songs to their king.'

John was standing next to the lady guide. He tapped her gently on the shoulder. 'Excuse me, Gerta,' he whispered to her – and, pointing to me, he said: '*He was there!*' Well, my goodness! I was asked to make a speech, and the group questioned me. The Americans made a fuss of me and took photos. Dearie me. Whit a cairry-on!

30

The General Assembly

It had always been my desire to be a commissioner at the General Assembly of the Church of Scotland. In 1992, the Kirk Session of High Carntyne Church invited me to have the honour of attending at the Mound in Edinburgh. I took my seat near the front of the action and was thrilled to join with 1,000 voices singing the opening hymn. I was doubly blessed in May of that year because, as well as having the privilege of being a commissioner in the great hall, I had the satisfaction of having my wee book, *The Glasgow Gospel*, published by Saint Andrew Press. Well, my goodness! It just seemed as if this kind of book was waiting to be done. One reviewer went well 'over the top' and described Jamie Stuart becoming a national celebrity overnight!

Interestingly enough, I had asked my friend the Reverend Hugh Wyllie to give me a foreword for the book, and he kindly obliged. Well now – lo and behold! – who was the new Moderator in the chair that first morning? Indeed – the Reverend Hugh Wyllie himself!

I was settled comfortably in my seat. Then it happened! I'll never forget the moment. The Lord High Commissioner for that year was Lord Macfarlane. He rose from his seat in the gallery (about six feet above the Moderator) and gave his address. His theme was the wealth of great cities, and he cited his own native city – Glasgow – as an example. He went on to praise Glasgow for its shipbuilding, car manufacturing and so on, and of course praised the greatest wealth that Glasgow possessed – the honest, hard-working Glasgow people. 'Yes, for sure – the people,' he exclaimed. 'Wealth indeed!' One doesn't get a standing ovation in the Assembly Hall, but Lord Macfarlane certainly got a sitting one.

Where was I? Oh yes! Then it happened! The Rt Reverend Hugh Wyllie stood up, turned round, looked up, smiled and replied to Lord Macfarlane: 'Thank you, Your Lordship. I agree with everything you say. As a Glaswegian myself, I know the wealth of the great city of Glasgow. In fact, sir, I have a present for you.' He then stretched his arm high and handed His Lordship a copy of *The Glasgow Gospel*. It's a moment I will always cherish.

Fast-forward twenty-one years to 2013 – and my church, once again, invited me to be a commissioner to the Assembly. At my advanced age, I knew many members of the Church of Scotland (including several former Moderators), and I looked forward eagerly to the important work of deliberations. On Monday morning, 20 May, I took my seat in the huge Assembly Hall. I now want to digress: as I sat in my seat before the proceedings commenced, my mind flashed back to August 1948 and the epic production of *A Satire of the Three Estates* in the Church of Scotland Assembly Hall. This, the most important play produced in Scotland before the twentieth century, was arguably the most significant pre-Shakespearean drama produced in the whole of the UK. Its influence on Scottish dramatic history has been immense, not least because, unlike most English drama of the time, it is as much an intervention in politics as it is a piece of entertainment. It asks serious questions about the Scots people, their heritage, history and about how the Scottish nation should be governed, and by whom.

Our 1948 production had run for three weeks to sell-out audiences. I played Sandy Solace, an inebriated courtier, who, along with others, was attempting to lead King Humanity into wicked ways. Sitting in my seat as an elder of the Kirk, I recalled Sandy Solace bursting through the entrance doors of the hall and running down the aisle, and – at the top of my voice – yelling: 'Wow! Wha saw ever sic a thrang? Methocht some said I had gane wrang! Had I help, I wid sing ane sang with a richt merry noise. I hiv sic pleasure in ma hert, I want tae sing the treble pairt! What is my name? Can ye not guess? Sirs, ken ye not Sandy Solace? They callit ma mither Bonnie Bess that dwelt aneath the bows. At twelve year auld she learnit to swive. Thankit be thee, great God of life – she made me faithers four or five!'

So, there endeth the digression – and I'm back in the twenty-first century! Now, I guess we all have a cause to support as we try to make the world a better place. For some years now, I have supported the Edinburgh-based Scottish charity ASH (Action on Smoking and Health Scotland). As a commissioner at the Assembly, I was aware that I would be allowed to speak if my theme was appropriate and could be slotted into the business of the day. I took advice from my friend, the Very Reverend Bill Hewitt, and he encouraged me to 'go for it'. On the Thursday of the Assembly week, the Church and Society Committee gave its report, and questions were invited. I was a wee bit nervous but, even so, put up my hand for permission to speak.

I got the nod from the outgoing Moderator, the Very Reverend Albert Bogle. The new Moderator, the Right Reverend Lorna Hood, had taken a tea break.

I was in the front row, and I stood up to my full height (nowadays five feet three inches)! 'Moderator, I want to raise awareness about the exploitation of tobacco farmers in developing countries by the tobacco industry. Our charity – Action on Smoking and Health Scotland – provides us with the facts:

The tobacco industry argues that it brings economic benefits to tobacco-growing countries. In fact, the majority of profits go to the companies, while the tobacco farmers often become trapped in a cycle of poverty and debt. Farmers are forced by the tobacco companies to enter into contracts to buy seeds and fertilisers at great cost. This does not even take into account the level of damage these chemicals cause when they end up in the soil, waterways and food chain. Child labour is also common, with poor families dependent on their children working in tobacco farms from an early age. The tobacco industry peddles a deadly and addictive product without a care for its consumers. I should also mention that the annual global death toll – at present, is 4 million. By the year 2030, that figure is expected to rise to 10 million, with 70 per cent of these deaths occurring in developing countries. Cigarette-smoking is the chief, single, avoidable cause of death in our society.

'Moderator, I am reminded of a famous work published 400 years ago, entitled *A Counterblaste to Tobacco*. It was written by my namesake, King Jamie Stuart, VI of Scotland and I of England. The final paragraph goes as follows: "Dear Countrymen, I declare, it is a habit loathsome to the eye, hateful to the nose, harmful to the brain, dangerous to the lungs, and in the black stinking fume thereof, nearest resembling the horrible Stygian smoke of the pit that is bottomless".'

Well – I got a 'sitting ovation', to be sure! The Very Reverend Albert Bogle stood up and declared: 'You have just heard from an elder who, at 92, is probably the oldest commissioner in the hall. That was a speech given with passion! We can use more of that. Now! Let that go out on the media!' Sure enough, my speech went out on BBC TV on the following Sunday. The Church of Scotland monthly magazine *Life and Work* is always very measured when giving reviews. Nevertheless, it said that the author of *A Glasgow Bible* made a speech that was 'well received'. What more could I ask?

31

A Happy Man

'Mr Stuart,' said the Girl Guide, 'the captain has asked us all to try to interview one of the older members of our congregation, and my mum suggested that I should speak to you. Well then, Mr Stuart, please tell me the story of your life, and I'll take some notes. First of all, can I ask if you are a happy man?'

How could I refuse such a plea? I gave the lassie some notes, and she seemed very pleased. 'Thanks, Mr Stuart. I'll call my story *A Happy Man*.'

That evening made me think about my life – and there sure were a lot of reflections. (Interestingly, I have also been invited to the Scottish Parliament to present the 'Time for Reflection' speech.) Was I a happy man? Yes indeed! I was a happy man. I was brought up in a Christian home, and I learned how to behave decently. I could not have asked for more caring parents.

I went to Sunday School and joined the Boys' Brigade. On joining the RAF, I was happy to be called a Christian.

However, during my five years on active service in an air crew, and seeing so much strife and sadness, my faith and belief in an Almighty God was sorely tested. I questioned myself about religion.

That all changed one Sunday morning in High Carntyne Church in the east end of Glasgow, where I lived and still do. My wife was a member of the church. I was not a member. The minister at that time was the Reverend James Martin. He preached a sermon which challenged me to the core. The theme of it was the dedication of the members of the Mormon Church at Salt Lake City, Utah, USA. Mr Martin told the whole story of how the Mormon Church (the Church of Jesus Christ of Latter-Day Saints) came into being, and then emphasised the strong dedication of the members.

'The tenets of the Mormon faith are strange to us,' he said. We would never accept them. However, we certainly cannot fault their deep devotion to their cause.'

He finished his sermon as follows: 'Well now, friends, as you sit here in God's house this morning, can you say you have a strong belief? Has Jesus entered your life? Why do you come to church? Is it just to be with your friends and sing the hymns? How do you really feel about Jesus? Can you honestly say that you accept Jesus as your Saviour? Are you searching for answers? If you are not sure about accepting Jesus, try this! *Leave the door open for him.* Ask him to come into your life.'

I had been struggling at that time with the reasons for my attendance at church. That sermon said it all: either I was willing to believe in Christ Jesus or I was not. I made a decision. That evening, in the stillness of my bedroom, I knelt down. 'Dear God,' I prayed, 'I want Jesus to come into my life.'

I did not see any bright lights, but I know in my heart that my thinking changed and I was prepared to embrace the Christian faith to the best of my ability.

I began to pray a lot, and I've been praying ever since. Does God answer prayer? I believe He does. Really? How about the Holocaust? How about wars and famines and earthquakes? Why doesn't an all-powerful God prevent these happenings? I don't know. The greatest theologians in the world cannot answer these questions.

For me, through my knowledge and faith in Jesus Christ, I believe that God is aware of everything happening in the world and that He is in control.

And, again, does God answer prayer? When my wife died over thirty years ago, I asked God to give me strength to come through my bereavement. I know that He answered my prayer. I thank God for His blessing and comfort.

And yet again – does God answer prayer? Yes, He does! I speak to God every moment of the day. Does He hear me?

I think back to my days as an actor. I realised it was not the life for me. I gave up the theatre and had no real regrets. I had learned a lot which would be to my advantage. What happened then? I couldn't find employment. In desperation, I took a job as a vacuum-cleaner salesman! Dear reader, that was a low point in my career. You should be playing sad violin music as you read this. I knocked on doors for four years, in the rain, in the snow – and in the hailstones! I prayed as I walked the streets. I prayed that, some day, God would use me in a worthwhile fashion.

Yes indeed, I prayed. Does God answer prayer? Twenty years later, with no literary experience, this wee vacuum-cleaner salesman, at the age of 71 years, penned *The Glasgow Gospel*. The book went to number one in the Scottish bestsellers' list and is now into its fifteenth reprint.

The days race on, and this book, *Still Running*, will be published (*Deo volente*) in September 2014 as I jog into my 95th year on this planet. What have I achieved? Have I changed anything? George Hoffman, the great British evangelist, wrote that one person cannot change the world, but *you* can change the world for one person.

I was speaking to a group of about 300 residents of Barlinnie Prison. After my presentation, one big chap came up to me. 'That wis dead brilliant, wee man, by the way. So it wis! See aw thae stories – the Prodigal boy and the Samaritan chap – were aw thae stories right fae the Bible?'

I assured him that they were all genuine Bible stories.

'Right then, wee man,' he smiled, 'I'm gonnae stert readin the Bible as from now!'

He asked to have my book, and I signed it for him. I hope he remembered to pack it when he signed off from the 'Bar-L'.

The Reverend John Hegarty gave good advice one Sunday morning. He preached to the effect that life is full of ups and downs. Then he said: 'If life is good for you, don't say you are lucky or fortunate, say you are blessed.'

Well, for sure, I've been blessed and no mistake! I've had a long, happy and exciting life, and I'm still going strong. I had a very happy marriage. I have two daughters, four granddaughters, one great-granddaughter – and one great-grandson!

I wish I could tell my story to my old teacher at Whitehill School.

A few years ago, my friend the Very Reverend David Lunan was in the pulpit in High Carntyne Church. Prayer was the theme of his sermon. We met at the end of the service and discussed the experience of prayer. I revealed to him that, on several occasions over the years, I had been very worried about something really important. I had then prayed, saying: 'Dear God, please help me'. I felt that, within a very short time, my prayers had been answered.

I related these happenings to David. He smiled and said: 'It's scary, Jamie, isn't it?'

Let me finish this 'Happy Man' story with my own rendering of the New Commandment:

The New Commandment

Jesus then took his disciples tae wan side and telt them, 'Ah'll soon hiv tae leave ye aw – an though ye search for me, ye canny follow efter. So listen, here's ma new command for ye: Ah want ye tae love wan anither, jist the wey I loved ye aw. That's the only wey that ye can prove tae folk that you are ma followers. There's nae greater love in aw the warld than this, that a man should lay doon his life for his freens. Don't let yer hert get heavy. Trust oan God – *trust oan me*. An mind, there are plenty rooms in ma faither's hoose. Ah'm gaun there tae prepare a place for every wan o ye. When things are ready, ah'll come back for ye, an we'll aw be thegither wance mair ...'

I reflect on this passage, and it gives me peace of mind. Surely we're all seeking to have comfort in our lives.

Psalm 139

Faither, you hiv tested ma hert, an ken everything aboot me.
You ken weel, baith when I sit doon, an when I rise.
You read ma dreams from far awa.

There isnae a word that leaves ma mooth, Lord, but you ken
ma drift.
I realise, Lord, that you are aw roon aboot me, an that you place
yer haun's blessin on ma heid.

Dearie me, Faither – this is too amazin tae believe!
Aye, where can I jouk frae yer spirit?
Where can I flee frae yersel?
If I nipped up tae heaven, you wid be there.
If I lay doon deid, you wid be there as weel.

If I flew on the wings o the mornin tae the deepest pairts o
the sea,
You wid find me there in a jiffy, an gie me the grip o yer haun.

If I pray that the mirk o the night shall cover me, even the mirk
isnae dark tae thee.

Dear Faither, you hiv created ma wondrous body, an knitted it
together in ma mither's womb.
I gie you thanks for makin me sae brilliant.

You kent me afore I was born, an planned each day o ma life afore I could breathe.
Every day wis pit doon in yer book.

How incredible, dear God, tae ken that you are thinkin aboot me aw the time.
I cannae even coont the times, an each mornin ye're cosy by ma side.

Oh blessed Faither o mine, let it be that you will examine me, an ken ma thoughts.
Check me for ma sins, dear God, an set me alang the road tae eternity.